BEHAVIOUR

BEHAVIOUR

The Lost Modules

Jen Foster

A Sage company
2455 Teller Road
Thousand Oaks, California 91320
(0800)233-9936
www.corwin.com

Sage
1 Oliver's Yard
55 City Road
London EC1Y 1SP

Sage
Unit No 323–333, Third Floor, F-Block
International Trade Tower Nehru Place
New Delhi 110 019

Sage
3 Church Street
#10-04 Samsung Hub
Singapore 049483

Editor: Amy Thornton
Development editor: Sarah Turpie
Senior project editor: Chris Marke
Cover design: Wendy Scott
Typeset by: C&M Digitals (P) Ltd, Chennai, India
Printed by CPI Group (UK) Ltd, Croydon CR0 4YY

Library of Congress Control Number: 2023933968

British Library Cataloguing in Publication Data

A catalogue record for this book is available from the
British Library

ISBN 978-1-5296-0873-1
ISBN 978-1-5296-0872-4 (pbk)

At Sage we take sustainability seriously. Most of our products are printed in the UK using responsibly sourced
papers and boards. When we print overseas we ensure sustainable papers are used as measured by the Book
Chain Project grading system. We undertake an annual audit to monitor our sustainability.

Contents

About the author   vii
Welcome to The Lost Modules: Start here   ix

1 What is behaviour?   1

2 Behaviour and language   15

3 Behaviour and connection   22

4 Behaviour and emotions   36

5 Behaviour and the classroom   53

6 Behaviour and rewards   69

7 Behaviour and learning   84

8 Behaviour and classroom management   95

9 Behaviour and consequences   107

10 Behaviour and trauma   123

11 Behaviour and bias   138

12 Behaviour and restorative practice   148

13 Behaviour and neurodiversity   159

14 Behaviour and you   173

15 Behaviour: The discovered modules   186

References   189
Index   194

About the author

Jen Foster is a fiercely passionate educator. She has been teaching for over a decade, including in a number of leadership roles. Jen has created a behaviour training pro- gramme that has been sold worldwide. Jen has an educational platform with a community of more than 80,000 followers. Jen is the founder of the first ever online Behaviour Encyclopedia: The Good Morning Club. She runs training sessions for schools and compa- nies and has written for the TES. Jen's resources support teachers with themes such as emotional literacy, wellbeing and behaviour. Jen's mission is to continue to learn and seek out the best strategies to support children and teachers to thrive. And after that? Share it far and wide.

Welcome to The Lost Modules: Start here

Allow me to introduce myself . . .

Oh hey! Thank you for being here. Let me introduce myself, shall I? My name is Jen Foster and, essentially, I am an educator. That's my jam. I guess you could say I am a particularly 'keen' teacher. I love what I do. I remember in my first ever interview I professed that I would still teach even if I won the lottery. Eleven years later, as cheesy as it sounds, I still feel the same way. A realisation struck me a few years ago that my level of enthusiasm may come across as excessive to some and might even be perceived as annoying. And by 'some', I do in fact mean my husband! We were teaching together abroad and I was excitedly sharing my Hansel and Gretel-themed maths lesson (which was 10/10 by the way!) on the drive home. Mid-recount he just turned to me ... 'Jen, I love you but I don't really want to talk about school right now.' OH SNAP! Some people don't want to talk about every detail of their lesson? WHO KNEW? It was that conversation that led me to starting a 'Teachergram' – an Instagram account dedicated to teaching content @goodmorningmsfosterltd. I started by just sharing everything and anything and loving having a community of keen beans like me. But it didn't take me long to spot something quite odd. Scrolling through thousands of teachers' experiences around the world there were two things that stood out like a sore thumb:

1. behaviour was this huge obstacle in teaching;
2. the guidance around behaviour was inconsistent, vague and unhelpful.

I started reflecting on my three-year Primary Education degree and, sure enough, I couldn't recall any clear and practical strategies. I just did what my placement teachers did. I raised my voice (pause to cringe); I used behaviour charts; I used class shops; I used detentions. I didn't bloody know. And what's worse, I didn't really think anything of it. I didn't think about the 'why' behind the behaviour management strategies I was using. I didn't question the pedagogy. I just mindlessly mirrored it. My classrooms on placement were controlled. I was praised for my behaviour management. I could 'run the room'. So if it ain't broke? You might be thinking the same. Why wouldn't you? You most likely are in the same boots I was. The 'in the dark', 'lack of training' dusty boots. Well, if you are, this book is exactly where you need to be because what I soon realised is those 'traditional' strategies used in schools contradict recent research (as well as common sense!).

So? I decided to learn everything I could about behaviour. I explored outside the education shelves and bought way too many books about neuroscience, positive psychology, business and parenting. The more I learnt, the more I reflected on my own practice and my own experiences in schools. SPOILER ALERT: My behaviour in school wasn't perfect.

I made it my mission to take everything I'd learnt (and continue to learn) and bring it to as many educators as possible in a jargon-free way. And here I am, with the opportunity to get all of those LOST MODULES down in a book of my own. Just to clarify, I am not a neuroscientist, psychologist, therapist or any other expert. Although I am a parent, this book is from an **educator** to an **educator**. As simple as that.

Why is there a need for this book?

Teaching is a lot. Did you know that teachers make 1,500 decisions a day? That's four decisions a minute (Klein 2021). That's more than a surgeon. Like, what? Experiencing 30 different needs all at once is exhausting. That's before we even get to the concept of managing them. Can we just give that some air time please? Can you give yourself a moment of absolute praise and recognition for how tricky this job is. Teachers choose to teach because we are genuinely and authentically driven to do it. We don't do it for the glam lifestyle of picking glue off our fingers. We don't do it for the money. (HA!) And we definitely don't do it for the mythical nine 'til three working day. We want to make a change. We are trailblazers, champions and frontline soldiers. No one is saying we don't want to do it. That is not the point. The point is: we actually didn't sign up for what we end up doing, which is firefighting. Teachers love what we do. So shouldn't we actually get to do it? And if behaviour is so all consuming and dominating, WHY THE HELL do we receive basically no training on it? Where are the modules on behaviour? Why did we go into the profession completely blindsided? AND WHY are we still waiting for adequate support? I created polls @goodmorningmsfosterltd asking educators their opinions on behaviour and this is what I found out:

93 per cent felt that they had inadequate behaviour training as a trainee teacher

88 per cent feel they have inadequate behaviour training as a qualified teacher

99 per cent believe behaviour has a negative impact on their teaching

98 per cent believe behaviour has a negative impact on their wellbeing

So isn't it about time we shined a spotlight on behaviour?

What I have included in this book and why

When writing this book I wanted to highlight all of the nuanced connections behaviour has with, well, everything! The thing is, behaviour is often just seen as a completely separate concept. But if you're only looking at behaviour, it's like being given glasses with no lenses. We will never actually see anything.

It's not *just* behaviour.

When we can truly understand the intersections of behaviour we can:

1. stop negative cycles;
2. reduce the ongoing behaviour incidents *drastically*;
3. understand rather than bang our heads against walls (leading to burnout, and you know, a sore head);
4. support our pupils to thrive well beyond the classroom.

Each **Lost Module** shares the connection with behaviour as well as actionable strategies. I have structured each chapter to be a digestible overview of the key concepts rather than taking you on a training course because I wanted it to be uncluttered and easy to read.

How to use this book

In order to really access the Lost Modules, it is important to be 'open' to them. Honestly, some information I learnt was a shock to the system. Some information is so against everything we are accustomed to and it can be tricky to process. Take your time and be open to the concept that there is more to discover.

I have added workbook activities throughout for a reason. Reflecting really helps us to understand, process and develop our perspective. I would recommend having a pen handy or at least stopping and actually thinking about the workbook questions before moving on.

Things to look out for:

- Foster Formulas – These are like my mindset mantras!
- Script snip – I will outline different scripts throughout.
- Takeaway bag – The headlines from the chapter.
- Lights, Camera, Action – These are your chapter reflections.

All together or take what you need

I wanted to create a structure where you can delve straight into a module and get immediate takeaways and strategies but, equally, you can read it cover to cover and build your mastery. It's up to you! Your reader's perspective was important to me so 'you do you' boo!

A note about you

The fact that you are reading this book tells me everything I need to know. You want to be the best teacher you can and you want to know and do better. How lucky we are to have you in this industry. You may read things in this book that you have done or are doing now. Guess what? Me too. This book isn't to shame you. This book isn't to criticise you. This book is all about bringing information YOU SHOULD HAVE RECEIVED into the forefront. Please know, we are in this together and we are all doing the best we can with the resources available to us.

DISCLAIMER 1: There is not a one size fits all strategy. Sorry. For bespoke and individualised behaviour support I would recommend seeking advice from the professionals in your school as they will be able to observe children and give expert recommendations.

DISCLAIMER 2: Learning is an ongoing process. Knowledge is always evolving and to be the best educators we can, we need to be open to new research and how it impacts our practice.

And with that, let's do this.

What is behaviour?

CHAPTER 1

In this chapter we are going to explore some of the things I wish I was taught about what behaviour actually is. This is my most visited chapter because, to be honest, what we know about behaviour is reflective of what we know in general. Neuroscience is (no surprise here) a complex concept and what we know about the brain is continually evolving. It can seem like you're navigating Middle Earth. But luckily, I had a helpful Gandalf guide in the form of Dr Emma Hepburn (Hepburn 2023) who helped me to debunk some myths around the brain.

So, before we talk about what behaviour is, let's just address what it *isn't*. There are so many vague ideas and myths about children's behaviour so let's just get to the root of that now.

Myths in schools

1. Despite what you may have been told, children are not deliberately trying to annoy you for the sheer purpose of bringing a bit of interest into their day.
2. Behaviour is not fully controllable.
3. And probably, most importantly, behaviour is not the child's issue or problem to figure out by themselves.

More myths in schools

1. Our brain is split into sections that work in isolated ways.
2. Our brain develops in isolated sections.
3. The amygdala is **only** in charge of our threat response.

(Hepburn 2023)

Oooh. If you're anything like me, some of those myths might have hit you sideways (and then across the face). I hear you. But as much as unlearning is so uncomfortable, using strategies that don't work is a whole new realm of frustration.

Before we move through this chapter – let's pause. I want you to think about a type of behaviour you presented as a child and how it was described by adults. Ooh. I know. You weren't expecting an activity so soon right? Ok, I'll go first. In primary school, I didn't participate. I think teachers would have called me 'lazy'. Ok your turn. Don't overthink it, just write a word in the box.

UNPICKING WHAT BEHAVIOUR ACTUALLY IS

_____

_____

_____

_____

_____

_____

_____

_____

Right, we will come back to that later. Now, let's take it to the books and explore what behaviour actually is. I feel compelled to remind you I am not a neuroscientist. Not even close, I got a C in Science GCSE. But you don't need a Harvard degree to learn about the brain and I really think every single teacher should be equipped with this information.

Behaviour is a neurological response

I'm not going to lie, the brain is super fascinating (and equally a place of mystery). But let's just take a tour of the pre-frontal cortex, hippocampus and amygdala. Although these aspects of the brain do not work in isolation (all of the brain is connected) it can be helpful to investigate key roles within the brain and what they are *generally* associated with. Each aspect is far more complex but for the purpose of simplicity:

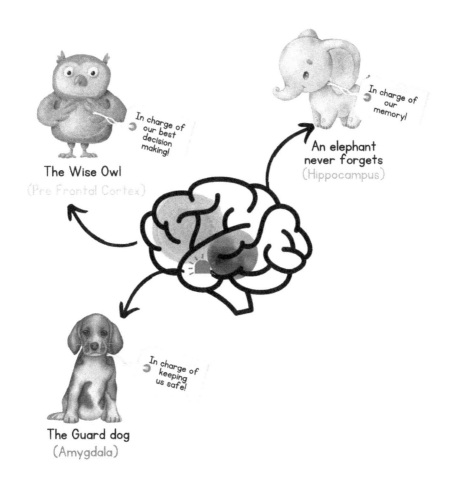

The Wise Owl
(Pre Frontal Cortex)
In charge of our best decision making!

An elephant never forgets
(Hippocampus)
In charge of our memory!

The Guard dog
(Amygdala)
In charge of keeping us safe!

The amygdala alarm meets the amygdala informant

The amygdala has many roles but it is most known for keeping us safe. I like to call it the guard dog. The amygdala plays a key role in the body's 'fight or flight' (although there are variations of this concept) survival responses. What basically happens here is our amygdala is like 'Ok, people there's a threat, everyone in positions.' Daniel Goleman called this 'the amygdala hijack' (Goleman 2020) with the idea that it shuts down key areas of the brain like the hippocampus and the pre-frontal cortex and takes control of our bodily responses, i.e. stress response. But Emma Hepburn shared a much better term: 'the amygdala inform-ant' (Hepburn 2023). Yes, the amygdala is sensing overwhelm in the body and that does link to our stress responses. Yes, our brain is driven by that sensation and overwhelm but it is not 'hijacked' and this doesn't mean emotions in themselves are irrational concepts. However, we can use 'the amygdala alarm' as an analogy to support us to understand how the brain is responding to the overwhelming emotion that is being experienced.

The amygdala alarm

This response isn't a bad thing. Like, if we were crossing the road and heard a screeching car sound round the corner we WANT our brain to respond. We don't want to weigh up our pavement choices and come to a rational conclusion of 'the safest side'. We don't need to recall the last three things on our to-do list right now. We don't need those areas of the brain. What we need is to react and to do it damn well quickly. So, the amygdala is not our enemy here. When a child (or ourselves) are feeling overwhelmed with emotions it might present in different ways. Scientifically speaking:

- your brain triggers signals that release the hormones cortisol and adrenaline, engaging your sympathetic nervous system;

- glucose is released into your bloodstream and fat is broken down to give you energy;

- breathing increases to get more oxygen in your body, your heart beats faster to pump blood faster, your pupils dilate, your thinking becomes more focused, senses sharpen and muscles tense. (Is that it?) ALL of this gets your body ready to respond to whatever action is required.

(Hepburn 2023)

Sometimes, guard dogs think there is a threat and they bark unnecessarily. Our brain is much the same. When our brain spots similarities in a situation (such as smell, sound, language used, tone, body language etc.) it is likely to respond in a similar way and over-predict for a threat. This is specifically important to note for our most vulnerable children.

The more prior experiences of threat, the more vigilant the brain becomes to predicting potential threats (Hepburn 2023). When we experience a threat response it looks different for different pupils. Here is an idea of what this response could look like in the classroom:

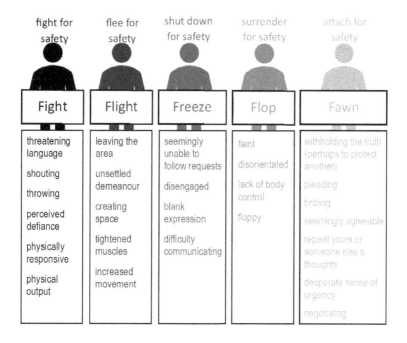

fight for safety	flee for safety	shut down for safety	surrender for safety	attach for safety
Fight	**Flight**	**Freeze**	**Flop**	**Fawn**
threatening language	leaving the area	seemingly unable to follow requests	faint	withholding the truth (perhaps to protect another)
shouting	unsettled demeanour	disengaged	disorientated	pleading
throwing	creating space	blank expression	lack of body control	bribing
perceived defiance	tightened muscles	difficulty communicating	floppy	seemingly agreeable
physically responsive	increased movement			repeat yours or someone else's thoughts
physical output				desperate sense of urgency
				negotiating

Why is this important? Because it takes us back to myth number 2. Behaviour is not fully controllable. As we get older we can self-regulate but both you and I know that task alone is WAY easier said than done. And to be honest, self-regulation is a lifelong pursuit. Now shift your perspective to your children and that mammoth task we expect them to do in a sensory-loaded classroom day. A final key point I want to make here is that our pre-frontal cortex, which is responsible for a variety of cognitive and executive functions such as planning, decision-making and impulse control, is not fully developed until around 25 years of age. GULP. We can't expect our pupils to control and manage their stress responses alone. On top of that, giving a child a punitive measure for being stressed doesn't really make sense now does it? Doesn't it seem like our system sets up our pupils and teachers to fail here?

What to take away from the amygdala alarm:

- Our emotions can cause a sense of overwhelm and impact our behaviour.
- Our threat system signals our brain to prioritise safety which means our body goes into 'fight/flight' involuntarily.

A handy model of the brain

Let's look at this with Dr Daniel Siegel's handy model of the brain (Payne Bryson and Siegal 2012). Although this does not correlate to most recent research of the brain, Emma Hepburn shares how we can use it as an analogy to help us notice and express our emotions (Hepburn 2023).

It works best if you act it out. Scrunch your hand into a fist but tuck your thumb in, got that bit? The thumb is the amygdala and your fingers are your pre-frontal cortex. The concept shows how they work great as a team but when our amygdala alarm goes off we quite literally 'flip our lid'. Go ahead, push your thumb against your fingers. Now you can see, our pre-frontal cortex is completely detached. All of those logical and rational decisions. Out the window. Now, our pre-frontal cortex is technically still attached to your head but the key takeaway here is we often try and 'reason', 'negotiate' or 'rationalise' with a child that is experiencing a stress response. They can't hear you (metaphorically speaking). The best way to support a child who has 'flipped their lid' is through regulation, de-escalation strategies and mindfulness. But more of that later!

You might have been in a situation where a child is throwing, shouting or running and you have tried talking to them. It seems like they aren't listening right? Because they cannot cognitively comprehend what you are saying at that moment as they are in a sense of overwhelm. Back to myth number 2: it is not fully controllable.

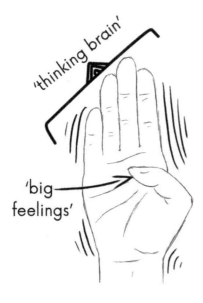

FLIPPED LID

You lose access to your 'thinking brain' which means your brain is operating from a place of fear.

CALM MIND

All parts of your brain are working in harmony.

What to take away from the hand model:

- The hand model can support us to notice if we have 'flipped our lid' when we feel a sense of overwhelm.
- It can help us express that feeling by literally saying 'I have flipped my lid.'
- It can also support us to associate our bodily sensations with our behaviour. 'I have flipped my lid because my heart is beating really fast.'

Behaviour stems from feelings and needs

The iceberg model

The iceberg model quite simply shows how behaviour is 'the tip of the iceberg'. The only thing we can see (Gilbert et al. 2021). But 90 per cent of what is going on is below the waterline – out of sight. That is the bit we need to reach. So what comes before that? Well, it all starts with our human needs and here we give a nod to our friend Maslow (Maslow 1943). If our needs are not met, we feel it. If those feelings are not supported or acknowledged they escalate, grow and manifest into behaviours. Emma Hepburn (Hepburn 2023) highlights how behaviour and emotions are intrinsically linked and it is our emotions that tell us what to do in a situation.

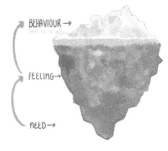

So, let's journey back to the word you wrote down earlier, about how your behaviour may have been described? Let's use the iceberg model to break down what was really happening there. I will go first. Some teachers may have thought my behaviour was lazy because I didn't participate. What were my feelings here? Well, more than anything, I was scared and confused. I really didn't know what was going on most of the time to be honest. So what were the unmet needs here? Safety. Am I going to get picked on to answer a question? Why don't I know the answer? Why does everyone else seem to know? All of these thoughts and a thousand more contributed to a low self-esteem problem which I desperately tried to hide by trying my best to be completely invisible. If my teachers knew that, how would it have changed the way they responded to me? I would imagine/hope that rather than rolling their eyes at my blank paper, they would differentiate the work for me and find a way for it to be accessible. So you see, there's a solution in sight when we dig a little deeper.

Your turn. Have a look at how I have broken down the iceberg model here to unpick that behaviour. You have a go with yours. It might take a while to think it through so take your time.

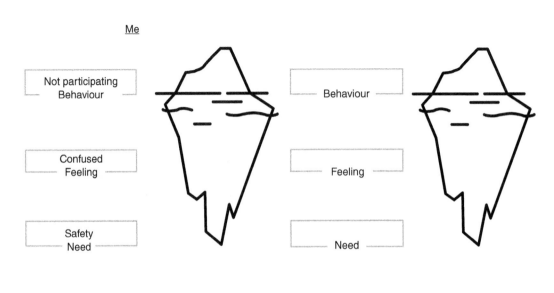

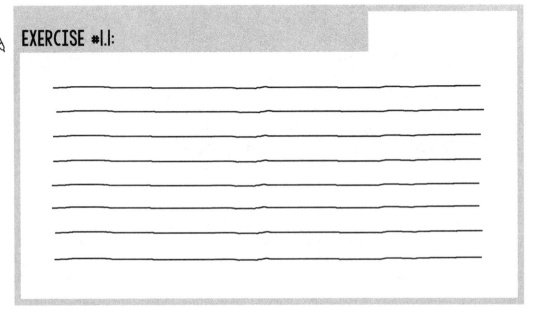

EXERCISE #1.1:

Foster Formulas

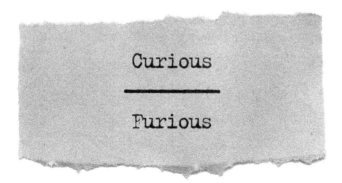

Being annoyed at 'what?' a child has 'done' doesn't help us to support them and it doesn't stop negative cycles. Finding out 'why?' is how we get to the root of the behaviour. When we do that we can put strategies in place that actually work rather than temporarily plugging the gap. So next time a child is presenting undesirable behaviours, look below the surface and ask why. That is a much more productive direction of thought. The problem here lies in the fact that we are not given enough time to genuinely and authentically support our children. There is so much pressure on extrinsic and numerical outcomes from our education system that it forgets what is really important. I'm not telling you **not** to be annoyed. But what I'm telling you is that being annoyed and showing you are annoyed is just the beginning. Because when we meet misbehaviour with misunderstanding we're both lost. It's a dead end. But when we meet misbehaviour with curiosity ... that, my friend, is a yellow brick road.

Disclaimer

Is it easy? No! I am not offering you a 'skip to the next level' hack. Having a Foster Formula and knowing the research isn't going to solve all your problems, but it is going to give you an idea of where to start.

STOP CALLING OUT LEWIS!

Ok, let me tell you about Lewis. Lewis would not stop talking on the carpet. I'm just going to say it like it is. He would not stop. He was calling out, he was talking to the people around him and sometimes he would even just be chatting to himself. I am going to be straight up real with you. For the first six weeks he was in my class I was reacting to that behaviour. I thought he was probably just testing boundaries. I thought I needed to be more consistent with my routine. It wasn't until six weeks had passed and I just thought 'Hmmm there is something else at work here.' So I started asking myself – why? I started looking at his behaviour more curiously. Was he calling out in every single lesson or was it more prominent in some lessons? Was there a focus to his talking or was it just random? Turns out, it was happening mostly in maths and English. And actually, he was mainly calling out the answers. So what was the root? He was bored. It was too easy. Aahhh. I caught up with his parents and yes, turns out Lewis was a little bit of a high flyer and was actually working about a year above (if not more!). If I didn't look beyond the behaviour, Lewis would probably have received consequences in line with the school system. That hits heavy for me and it takes me back to myth number 1. We need to banish the thought that children are *just* behaving a certain way for the sake of it.

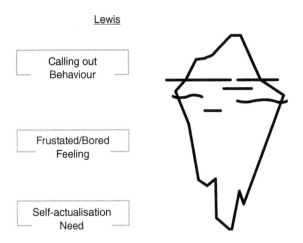

Lewis

Calling out
Behaviour

Frustated/Bored
Feeling

Self-actualisation
Need

STOP REFUSING OLIVER!

Oliver was often quiet but would have moments of complete refusal. He would walk out. Hide under desks. Throw things. He would be seemingly unresponsive to any instruction or direction from me. I naturally found this quite stressful. I tried to be firm, hold the boundaries. When his behaviours were extreme it was out of my hand and he ended up in punitive measures with senior leaders. It seemed to me like he was in a threat response. But it seemed sporadic and I couldn't identify any obvious triggers. It was a real head scratcher for me and every week the cycle continued. Until our rota changed and I needed to teach PE once a week. And then it all became so clear. It was happening on the PE days. Oliver was so self-conscious and so embarrassed that he did everything he could to get out of PE. He self-sabotaged. He was doing everything within his control to avoid that feeling of shame because he felt like he was terrible at PE. There was no quick fix here. Once I knew, the only thing I could do was focus on building his self-esteem. I tried to incorporate PE-style activities into more lessons to normalise this and made PE as informal as possible. Did his behaviour change overnight? Absolutely not. But did his behaviour improve? 100 per cent. The more extreme behaviours became rarer and rarer and my connection with him became stronger. This brings us to myth 3. Children can't just figure it out by themselves. They need a trusting and invested adult to support them and provide strategies. Just like we wouldn't expect a child to just figure out how to read. We need to have the same mindset when it comes to behaviour.

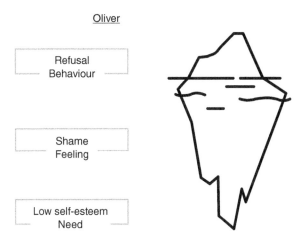

Oliver

Refusal
Behaviour

Shame
Feeling

Low self-esteem
Need

WELL DONE REBECCA!

In schools there is a general consensus that the goal is compliance. If a child is sitting, looking and seemingly listening you're doing the right thing. No further questions your honour. But compliance isn't the goal and underneath compliance are some pretty complex feelings and needs. We want our children to enjoy learning and to celebrate themselves as individuals. Rebecca was super quiet and compliant for about twelve weeks of school. However, she then became increasingly anxious. Below that veneer of compliance was a child who was incredibly nervous and just wanted to do the right thing. As one anxiety slipped out of the net it was honestly a real-life 'can of worms' situation. There were so many parts of her school and personal life that were worrying her and it became overwhelming for her. Mostly, she felt like she wouldn't be accepted for showing her true thoughts. She couldn't join the classroom and felt visibly distressed. It was such a shock for all the adults because we just didn't see it coming. I worked through this anxiety with Rebecca through buddy circles, utilising sensory tools, the calm space and

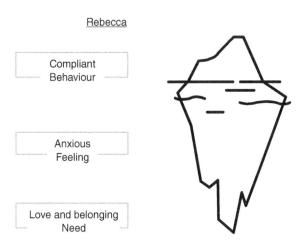

Rebecca

Compliant
Behaviour

Anxious
Feeling

Love and belonging
Need

home–school interactions. What came out of this was the true Rebecca. She was so out-going, so funny, and truly herself. And that, that was absolutely priceless to be a part of. So the moral here is even compliance needs unpicking and linking back to myth 2. Seeking to control behaviour never ends well!

I wanted to leave a workbook example here for you to unpick a child's behaviour you have been thinking about. You can do it now or come back to it when you get struck by behaviour bafflement!

EXERCISE #1.2:

_____

_____

_____

_____

_____

_____

_____

_____

Child:

| Behaviour |

| Feeling |

| Need |

Takeaways from the iceberg model

- It is never 'just behaviour'.
- Being curious about the root of the behaviour can support us to predict or understand behaviour.
- Being curious about the root of behaviour can help us to proactively support needs and feelings.

Behaviour is nuanced

Using what we know about the brain, needs and feelings, we might assume the phrase 'All behaviour is communication'. Which, in fairness, I like. I like the idea behind it but it can sometimes be problematic. Let's think about ourselves. Have you ever said 'I honestly have no idea why I did that?' Now, yes, there might be an underlying reason that you don't know yet. But, it is a very complex thing isn't it? Sometimes trying to understand what we do and why we do it is like falling down the rabbit hole! To then try and unpick 30 needs and minds in our class can seem a bit of a headache to say the least. The task isn't to know all the answers. The task isn't to spend our evenings trying to figure it out. Just the knowledge and understanding that behaviour is nuanced is what we need in education. I know that's not what you want to hear and you were probably hoping for a cheat sheet. But the truth is, behaviour is far more than a cheat sheet. *The Lost Modules* is all about uncovering the different connections behaviour has!

Takeaways

- There are no cheat sheets.
- Knowing the connections between behaviour and everything else can help us to truly support pupils and ourselves.

And that takes us to the end of this chapter. It is probably a chapter you will revisit again (I know I do!). I hope it has equipped you with the knowledge and confidence to really understand behaviour as we continue to move through the lost modules!

TAKEAWAY BAG

- Behaviour is more than just 'behaviour'.
- Behaviour is intrinsically linked to emotions.
- Behaviour is a neurological and physical response.
- Behaviour is nuanced as hell!

LIGHTS, CAMERA, ACTION REFLECTION

LIGHTS

What stood out to you in this chapter?

CAMERA

What does this look like for you right now? Tomorrow?

ACTION REFLECTION

What do you want to learn more about? What do you want to develop further?

CHAPTER 2

Behaviour and language

I'm going to ask you to do a few things in the chapter. Ergh, I know, doing things? Unacceptable. You were probably just hoping to have a little chilled read right? SOZ! But, in all fairness, I did warn you. Ok, so now we are all on high alert and ready to be picked on in class, I can begin!

I want you to have a little trip down memory lane. A little scan of your brain. I want you to think about a time a trusted adult said something *to* you or *about* you. In the last chapter we had an instinct reflection on how our behaviour may have been described in school. But, now I want you to think about something that has really **stuck** with you. Something that you really FELT. And maybe, to this day, you still do. It might be something that comes back into your mind every now and again. *Ok, try your best not to skip forward. Play along, you little troublemaker. Have you got it? Write it below:*

EXERCISE #2.1:

_____

_____

_____

_____

_____

_____

_____

_____

I am going to make a wild guess that it was something negative. Am I right? Read back, did I say the word negative or unhappy? Nope. (Note: if it was a positive experience. I am genuinely happy for you.) What I want to say next is all about encouraging that mindset for our teachers and children. Have you heard of negative bias? It is this really annoying way our brains are wired that just means we remember and focus on the negative things more than the positive (Moore 2019). We hold on to them. We believe them. A teacher once told me it takes twenty good comments to outweigh a bad comment. I don't know if that is an actual statistic, but it kind of makes sense to me.

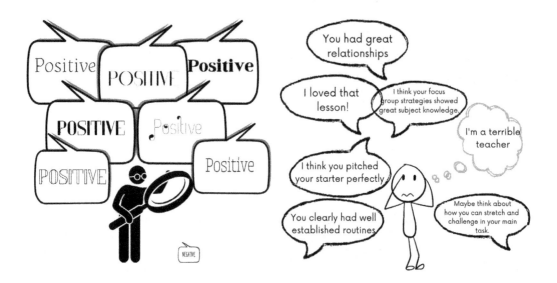

Since you shared, I'll share too. A teacher once said to me, 'You are one of the failures of the year.' Pause for gasps. I felt that. I still feel that. The thing is, words matter. Language matters. What we say to children, what we say about children, it impacts how we support them and how they feel supported. One comment can be the difference between getting in the race and throwing in the towel. And that is a lot. But the problem is, we have a lot of outdated language in education. Especially, when it comes to behaviour. You might think, Jen, come on. Are you really going to dedicate a chapter to language? Does it really make a difference? And my answer will be HELL YES. Language can have a huge impact on our instinctive thoughts and feelings (Shashkevich 2019). Words build from experiences, fleeting moments, unsaid thoughts and become incredibly powerful. Don't believe me? Buckle up, for round two of our next game. I'm going to give you a few words and I want you to write about what thoughts and feelings come to mind. Add them in the box on the next page.

I want to apologise for bringing up thoughts of an observation. That was mean. But you felt something right? You had an immediate thought right? But guess what, let's continue this language ride because we are on a roll, my friend. We can also argue that language also impacts action (Weimer 2015). Language can influence how we respond to a situation. For example, if we are told a child is lazy, we might be a bit more 'alert' to them.

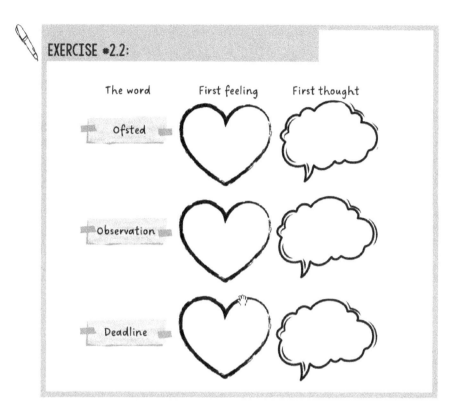

EXERCISE #2.2:

The word	First feeling	First thought
Ofsted		
Observation		
Deadline		

We might check their book first when we are marking. We might pull them up on the carpet more. If we are told a child is rude, we might have our back up a bit. We may be looking to assert our authority quickly and more prominently. You see, when we label children we are often sealing an envelope for their fate. WOW, that sounds uber dramatic right? But think about it. We ALL know children who have had labels that they never seem to shake off. HELL, I was one of them. The 'failure', the 'underperformer', the 'quiet' one. You will be very well versed in my previous labels by the end of this book! Here is some of the language we are currently using in schools (either willingly or unwillingly):

- lazy
- manipulative
- attention seeking
- low-level behaviour
- challenging behaviour

Wittgenstein famously wrote that:

    The limits of my language stand for the limits of my world.

                                                    (Wittgenstein 1933)

Well, I'd like to (humbly) adapt this to:

> The limits of our language stand for the limits of our education.

When we change the way we talk about children, we change the way we think about children. It removes this invisible barrier of supporting a child. It removes that damaging stamp and allows every child to be given a fresh slate to flourish. It allows us to look at a child as a child. Rather than a problem. So what words do we need to change and why? This list is not extensive. The replacements are also not engraved in stone. These are just ideas. Food for thought. I want to insert a little disclaimer here that this is a SAFE SPACE about moving forward. About unlearning and learning together to do the best for our children. I don't want you to go down a road of *Game of Thrones* shame. We have all said or done things we aren't going to write a family newsletter about but this isn't about the past. It is about the future. Y'all ready? Let's do it.

Lazy = Struggling to access or apply

When we reframe this, we are no longer blaming the child. We suddenly have actional next steps. Why are they not actually doing the work? Is there a way we could differentiate it differently? Could we try a different learning partner? Are they struggling with stamina or concentration? Would a checklist be helpful? Suddenly, we have a plan or at least a train of thought that could possibly lead to a plan!

Manipulative = Struggling to trust adults

When we are told a child is manipulative, we might be suspicious or cautious of them. When we are told a child is struggling to trust adults, we immediately feel a sense of empathy. What has happened to this child which has meant they cannot trust adults? What difficulties are they facing? How can I be their champion? We WANT to support them rather than dread being around them.

Attention seeking = Connection seeking

Attention seeking? How annoying. What a pest. It's you vs the class clown. Connection seeking? Well that just makes everything so much simpler doesn't it. If you know a child is seeking connection, your action and strategy is in the name. Give it to them. Acknowledge them. Meet that need. I am not saying it is a magic wand. But it is a magic mindset. One that activates positive action.

Low-level behaviour = Unsettled behaviour

I don't know about you. But I have taught through this era of 'low-level behaviour' and it drives me mad. I remember a very prominent and unhelpful Ofsted article describing low-level behaviour as 'idle chatter' or 'disturbing other children'. How does that help us? How does that give us any idea as to what we can do? All it does is blame children and teachers while providing zero insight. Well no thanks babes. NO THANKS. I am not saying these behaviours do not happen. What I am saying is we need to reframe. What is happening? If children are talking or fidgeting, they are displaying unsettled behaviour. This then gives us an ACTUAL indication as to how they might be feeling and what they might need. Are they bored? Can they access the work? Do they feel a bit restless or tired? Each of these questions naturally lead us to possible strategies such as movement breaks or differentiation. Boom, it doesn't feel so downright irritating now. It seems like more of a challenge. More of a mission to solve.

Challenging behaviour = Distressed behaviour

For me, challenging behaviour is a trigger. If I am told I have a defiant or challenging child I feel a bit on edge. The same way I might feel if there was an intoxicated man outside my house. It feels a bit ... threatening. WHY are we talking about children like this? When we use this term we are drawing an invisible battle line. Us vs them. We are making them out to be the villain. At the end of the day, a child is a child. We are educators. So what we need is language that helps us understand the behaviour and strategies that actually work. What we don't need is just to have a child in our class we have no idea what to do with. When we say distressed behaviour we are addressing the needs and feelings. Someone who is happy and calm is not likely to shout or swear in your face. Someone who is feeling regulated is unlikely to knock a table over. So when we are looking at the feelings instead of the behaviour we can at least begin to understand it. This shift in language helps us move from butting heads all year to finding a way.

Is = Is presenting

We often fleetingly use the word 'is'. This child is unsettled. This child is distressed. That isn't actually who they are. So even when we make changes to the terms, we also need to make changes to the structural language. I know, super linguistic and techy over here. But when we change 'is' to 'is presenting' we are disassociating the behaviour from the individual. Which is a more helpful way of thinking, i.e. the child is presenting unsettled behaviour.

Language is so often overlooked as an influencing factor in schools. For me, I try and reflect as to whether the language is helping me to support a child or providing a hindrance. If I feel like a conversation about a child's behaviour has hit a dead end, it might be because the language has created an obstacle. Shifting how we talk about behaviour is a key component in shifting our mindset.

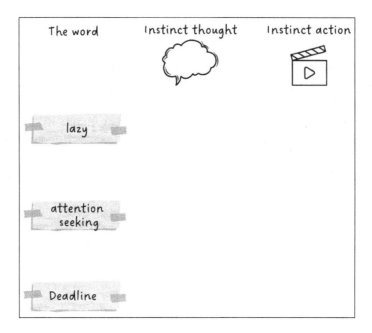

And so we come to the end of our journey through language. Hopefully, it has sparked some reflection and insight into the terminology around behaviour. The language I learnt in training is still being circulated today. So let's bring this out of the shadows and into our classrooms.

TAKEAWAY BAG

- Language can influence our thoughts.
- Language can influence our actions.
- The language we use around behaviour may be creating unnecessary obstacles.

LIGHTS, CAMERA, ACTION REFLECTION

LIGHTS

What stood out to you in this chapter?

CAMERA

What does this look like for you? What words are you bining?

ACTION REFLECTION

Are there any other words you are questioning? What do you think might happen if the education system shifted to this language reframe?

CHAPTER 3

Behaviour and connection

This chapter is about the ever elusive 'teacher–pupil relationships'. Why they matter and how we can actually build them.

I have already shared some ponderings from my past and this chapter is no different. This time I want to talk about 'The Likeability Factor'. In primary school, I didn't feel like I was likeable. I felt like I wasn't good enough. I felt this way because of the sheer lack of connection I had with my teachers. I remember my mum reading my report card, it was so vague. She was like, well this doesn't tell me anything? It's like they don't even know you. I was craving connection but I didn't know how to get it so instead I was just silent. I became a shell of the person I could have been. I spent most of my time thinking about how I could be like the other children. The children the teachers clearly loved. This didn't just impact my connection with school. It impacted my progress and my attainment. I remember being removed from the singing assemblies and going to a small room doing maths and I remember the tired look on the teacher's face as I once again had the wrong answer. I remember constantly feeling confused and trying to mask this. I guess that's why this chapter is really dedicated to young Jen more than anyone else. Because she's the reason I became a teacher. I wanted every child to feel seen and to feel special and that just being their true authentic self is the most beautiful thing in the world.

What Mr Hetty taught me

There's always one isn't there? Everyone has that one champion. That teacher that just got it. For me, it was Mr Hetty. I met Mr Hetty in Year 9 and by this time I was well and truly done with the education system! I really had a lack of interest and care and didn't see a place for myself. Now Mr Hetty didn't do an outlandish act of love or connection. Because relationships don't work like that. There wasn't one memorable moment that changed my attitude towards education. It was small subtle acts of connection. Giving me personal feedback about my work, really listening when I was talking, following up with me if I didn't seem myself, asking about my family. It was an accumulation of kindness that ultimately just made me feel seen. And what Mr Hetty taught me is it only takes one person. It only takes one teacher that genuinely believes in you. So, you know what I'm going to ask don't you? *Who was it for you? Is there a teacher that is the reason YOU became a teacher? Is there a teacher who was your champion? Who is the one that you will never forget, and why?*

EXERCISE #3.1:

_____

_____

_____

_____

_____

_____

_____

_____

Here's what really bugs me about relationships in schools. Ever since I started teaching, 'relationship' has been this word that comes up all the bloody time. Build your relationships. Maybe it's your relationships? Don't forget your relationships! Now, what I'm **not** saying is that relationships are not important. Obviously, they are super important which is why we are here loving life in this chapter. What I **am** saying is why do people keep telling us about relationships but do not give any time to actually build them? Why are we told to develop relationships but not given ideas about how to do that? How come relationships become this accountability for teachers without any prior support? I have found it very irritating because relationships are an essential part of teaching. They are not an afterthought and they have an undeniable impact when it comes to behaviour, wellbeing and learning.

Let's take it to the books

So, what does the research actually say about relationships and where are we finding that evidence-based back-up? I want to introduce Robert Waldinger. He is kind of a big deal because he is a psychiatrist that conducted the longest ever study about human happiness and guess what? (Waldinger 2015) It is still going on! It is 80 years strong and it keeps on going. What I love about this study is it makes everything so simple and it supports us to really reflect on how misconstrued our outlook on life can be. As part of this study, they asked millennials what their big life goals were. Do you know what they said? 80 per cent of them said that one of their biggest life goals was to be rich and a whopping 50 per cent said they wanted to be famous. But, the results from the 75-year study could not be clearer. In order to be happier and healthier we need connection. Period. I can't help but think we are missing the mark in schools.

We can't change behaviour until we change connection.

(Kennedy 2022)

Last year, I was working as a school leader and a classroom teacher. As a school leader I had many responsibilities and this meant I had a lot of time out of class. Sometimes even three afternoons a week. What I noticed when I came back into class was a little short of chaos! Children were unsettled, children were out of routine and clearly felt a sense of detachment. This all showed in their behaviour. They weren't listening, working together, following instructions and it was difficult. Here's the thing, instead of ploughing through with my lesson plan and constantly correcting and reprimanding children. I just stopped. I focused on us. I had been away from my class and they had felt it. So the most impactful and powerful thing I could do was to tap into that connection. And when I did? We were back on track baby.

Dr Kennedy uses a piggy bank analogy that I love! She says to imagine that we all have a piggy bank. We can equate a full piggy bank to positive mental health and wellbeing. When our piggy bank is full, we are thriving and at our best. Here's the thing, the currency is connection (Kennedy 2022). Our behaviour is responsive to our piggy bank status because it impacts our responses.

For example, let's say my husband and I had an amazing date night and then we missed the bus we were planning to get. Boohoo right? It's nothing to write home about. We'd probably giggle our way into a long walk (or, you know, an Uber!). But, let's say we had a huge argument. Let's say we were in tears and then we missed that bus. Suddenly, that seems like more of an event. At the time, it feels like nothing is going right. And our responses and behaviour following it will likely escalate.

So, let's put this idea into the context of behaviour in schools. If a child's piggy bank is looking a little depleted, we will see it in behaviour. Because ultimately, behaviour stems from a lack of connection and/or an unmet need. When our piggy bank is full to the brim, our behaviour is more settled which means we are more content, focused and able to be our best selves. As our finances dwindle, so does our tolerance and emotional resilience.

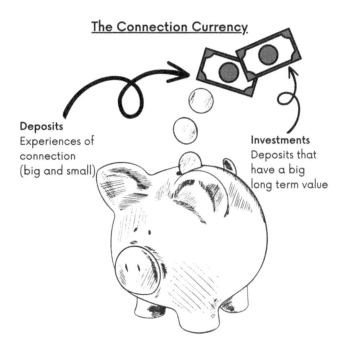

The Connection Currency

Deposits
Experiences of
connection
(big and small)

Investments
Deposits that
have a big
long term value

Piggy bank daily deposits

So, let's talk deposits. I am so done with the generalised advice. What can connection look like for you and your class? Daily deposits are like connection coins we can use daily to support our pupils to feel a sense of love and belonging.

Deposit: Build connection with food
Action: Eat lunch with your class

Research shows that eating together builds social connections because it happens in an informal environment and provides a topic to naturally talk about! (Ageing Better 2019). We can all relate to being at a potentially awkward dinner and drawing for the: 'So, how is your food?' Sometimes, the classroom can seem very much your turf. Hanging out with your children in a mutual environment feels a bit safer and therefore they are more likely to be at ease. I am not telling you to give up your lunch everyday. That AIN'T me. But this is a great connection coin and here's how you can cash it in:

- Find out what time they are in the hall.
- Tell your class you're going to eat with them and you can't wait.

- Come and sit with them and join in 'their' conversation rather than making it feel like a lesson.
- Be genuine and listen to whatever stories they want to tell you.
- You can't sit with every child but you can smile or wave at as many as you can.
- Enjoy yourself!

Deposit: Build connection on their turf!
Action: Get yourself to the playground

The playground is their territory. This is where it all happens. You coming into their space means you are the guest! It means they are naturally more confident and likely to open up and be at ease. Let's not forget that being outdoors has its own wealth of benefits for wellbeing. When we combine that with social connection we are on to a winner. Once again people, don't give up your time. But popping out five minutes earlier can really make a world of difference. Let's cash it in:

- Simply come out to play five to ten minutes before the bell will ring.
- Find your kids and join in with whatever they are doing.
- Let them take the lead.
- Ask them questions about 'how to play' and what you can do.
- They will probably flock to you! Try to acknowledge them with hugs and smiles!

Deposit: Build connection with oxytocin
Action: Sing with your class

I know what you're thinking. Jen, babe, no. Or, I am not a singer girl. You don't need a personality transplant and no matter who you are or what your personality may be – singing with your class is for YOU. Singing together is a shared experience that creates a bond! (Keeler et al. 2015). It's unspoken, but we all feel its magic. It makes us one voice united together, it's just special! There's an increasing amount of evidence that singing releases endorphins, serotonin and dopamine – the 'happy' chemicals that boost your mood and make you feel good about yourself. And let's be real, singing has proven time and time again to be one of the most effective and engaging attention getters because people WANT to be involved! Don't agree? Just play 'Sweet Caroline' in your next staff meeting or observe everyone pretending they know the words to 'auld lang syne' at New Year. (I literally had to Google the name but HELL if I won't sing along!) I remember I had one of those notorious 'tricky' classes and after lunch time was a nightmare. They were so dysregulated and there was so much play time friction. I felt like it took forever to actually start the after-noon. One day, I just put a Bruno Mars song on as they came in and started singing.

It became our tradition. We would sing together for ten minutes or so after lunch and the mood boosting was undeniable. It was such a special time for me seeing their little faces light up! Let's cash in that coin:

- Have a singing routine like a tidy up song!
- Create a singing routine like having a class song that you sing after lunch or before the end of the day.
- Use songs to punctuate your day.
- Sing your instructions!
- Put a child friendly playlist on Spotify.
- Use songs for learning.
- Let the video do the singing! You don't need to take centre stage, just put on the lyrics and sing along.

Deposit: Build connection with endorphins
Action: Move!

Research around 'myokines' (Hickey 2022) and 'the feel better effect' (Pillay 2016) shows that when we move in a room altogether simultaneously this strengthens connection and releases chemicals in the brain that helps you access this sense of connection (Mayo Clinic 2022). Think about images of Woodstock (69 not 99!), that festival vibe when everyone is in the same place, hearing the same thing, moving at the same time. It is a THING. We feel it. We have to remember that movement is a type of communication. We curate movements that specifically communicate kindness, connection and co-operation such as hugging or shaking hands. That is why 'ice breakers' tend to involve movement (much to our dismay)! You can cash in this coin whether you are a professional dancer or an incredibly unfit adult like myself! Here's how:

- It can be as simple as having a mid-lesson stretch!
- A daily (or hourly) yoga pose.
- Use the Emotions Toolbox and pick a movement video to do with your children.
- Have fun with it! If your kids want to do the macarena or Candy, just enjoy it! This shared experience is what it's all about.
- Embed it into your routines like a song for tidying or a morning move and groove!
- Build it into your lesson, could you add a grammar dance or times table aerobics workout?

Piggy bank investments

Often when we talk about relationships it can seem quite one-dimensional, it's like ok do *this* and you will get *that*. We know that isn't the case though don't we? Relationships are multifaceted. Daily connection coins are actionable tools for developing your pupil relationships but we can also make connection investments. These are habits and rituals that we can do all the time to continually strengthen our relationships with our pupils. Think of them as notes instead of coins because they have a different kind of value.

Investment: Build connections with acknowledgement
Action: Greetings

Children need to be 'seen'. If you don't have a positive interaction with them first thing in the morning, it might be 30 minutes, an hour or MORE until they actually get 1:1 air time with you. This can have an immediate impact on feeling 'seen' and their sense of belonging in your class. Research shows that greetings are one of the basic functions of communication and trigger positive conversations. It helps us connect to people at a more personal level. You might be wondering:

Where would I stand? How will the children come in? What will they do if I'm not in the class?

Here are some suggestions and ideas to help you through that process if this is something new for you.

- If you have a teaching assistant, amazing! They can stay in class with the morning task while you stand at the door and greet every child.
- If you don't have one, don't worry! You just need a really predictable and consistent morning routine so it runs itself!
- The morning task requires thought because you don't want to be panicking or feeling overwhelmed. Morning set-up is everything. I normally had a journalling prompt on the board or children would come in and read.
- There are lots of ways to greet your children so make it work for you! It is important that it reflects your personality and your style!
- If you don't get to every child don't beat yourself up! You've always got the register 'Oh Jen, I didn't see you this morning. It's so great to see you.'
- When greeting each child, take their lead! They may want to have a little natter, they might just want a smile and a 'So happy to see you here today!'
- Aim to give everyone a genuine smile and good morning. Take the time to stop and give them your undivided attention, even for just a minute. What a great way to start their day.

Investment: Build connections with empathy
Action: Reading

I am a huge advocate for reading. Just ask my husband who is continually annoyed with me and the mini library I have created in our small London flat! The thing is, when we listen to stories it activates our limbic system (Lastiri 2021) which is the part of the brain associated with feelings. It means children are genuinely connecting with us! It is a community-building activity. Regardless of your age. Research shows that when we are listening to a story and following along with a plot it actually has a physiological impact (Cell Press 2021). Our heart rate syncs up with those around us as we listen together. There's some evidence from neuroscience (Pearce 2019) which suggests that when I'm telling you a story and you're listening to my story, our brain patterns begin to mirror one another. We are connecting, and the empathy is on not just an emotional but a physical level. It creates a shared experience. You can gab about a character or laugh out loud together. Relationship building happens through experience. Storytelling creates those experiences! And you can find a story FOR JUST ABOUT ANYTHING! Here's how I invested in reading as a full-time class teacher:

- Carve out the time. Actually plan it in. I decided I would do it before dismissal and I did.
- I'm not going to lie. Some days I just felt like I didn't have the energy to pull up a chair and do a dramatic reading. But what I realised is, reading a story is one of the best classroom management tools because everyone is listening. Just start and you'll see!
- Make sure everyone can see the book. Sounds obvious but easier said than done! A visualiser is magic!
- Try and look at children while you are reading. This is great for that connection!
- Can children join in? Can they finish the sentence? Can they make that sound too? The more involvement the better!
- Try and read the book first before reading it to your class. This means you can 'perform' it better. Kind of like a lesson plan I guess!
- If you feel like your class needs a 'busy hands' option, let them draw on a whiteboard as you read. This is a lovely comprehension activity. Children can then share their drawings and discuss similarities.

Investment: Build connections with fun and imagination!
Action: Play

Play **is** communication. Play is one of the ways we can connect and one of the primary ways our children connect! Sharing laughter is going to hack our happy hormones (Robinson et al. 2022) which is what it's all about really isn't it? Cultivating experiences of happiness with our children. Being playful is essential in building and maintaining awesome, healthy bonds. It turns out playfulness and silliness are related to greater relationship satisfaction, increased feelings of trust between people, and stronger connections. Now playing doesn't necessarily mean that you have to play an actual game every day. But, to be honest I do love playing a game every day! Play is so much more than that! Play is a way of communicating and you can integrate the essence of play into absolutely anything. Disclaimer: play is for every age. Here's some ideas:

- Playing while reading a story.
- Playing outdoors – Take a lesson outdoors or join them for five minutes outside!
- Playing a learning game – This could be a Topmarks or Wordwall game or a no resource game!
- Explorative play – Get the Lego/play-dough/Connectix out. Yes children will still want to do this in Year 6! Hell, adults bloody do. Oh … and have fun with them!
- Team-building games – Get the parachute out. Need I say any more?

Investment: Build connections with positive feedback
Action: Character compliments

There are lots of different types of compliments. Here are some common ones we may give to children.

APPEARANCE

I love your hair!

OUTCOME

Well done for finishing all of the questions!

GENERIC

You're amazing!

CHARACTER

Wow, you were so resilient today! Well done for pushing through those challenges!

Really, what we all want, in ANY relationship is to feel seen and valued for who we really are. Not what we did, not what we wore, not what we said, **who we really are.** Positive psychology tells us that we all possess 24 character traits (Seligman 2011). (Although, every individual has their own set of character strengths.) When we praise character we are praising something that children can develop and grow rather than something they can win or lose at. It is likely you have noted how praise develops relationships. But character praise is much more powerful because it shows how much time you've taken to observe and get to know them which links back to that investment in our children.

INSTEAD OF...   TRY...

You're doing the      I love how you're
right thing well   leading your team.
done.   You're great at
                                                        encouraging others!

You've got your   I love your energy! You
hand up well done.   always put your all
                                                        into everything!

A great idea!   I love how your mind
Good job!   always thinks outside
                                                        the box. You're so
                                                        creative!

- Don't worry about trying to get 'the perfect praise' every time. It can be hard to get in the swing of it. I just try and **pause** before praising and think about what dispositions and attitudes they showed. Early years teachers are amazing at this because they observe before interacting.
- Try describing the **process** instead of the outcome. 'You really persevered through that maths work! Well done!'
- Thanking the character trait. 'Thank you for being so patient.' 'Wow thank you for that interesting question.'

Investment: Build connections with meaningful questions
Action: No more 'How are you?'

How are you?

Good, you?

Sound familiar? Yep. We are all guilty of it! Although every single one of us has good intentions, how are you, just isn't hitting the mark! No, I am not cancelling 'How are you?' But I am saying there are some alternatives that can have a big impact in terms of teacher/pupil connection! Instead of asking 'How are you?' Try asking:

- What colour are you today?
- What shape are you now?
- Which emoji best describes your mood?
- What genre of music are you today?
- What would be your song title today?
- Which book character best describes your mood?
- What mythical creature are you today?
- What type of weather best describes your mood?
- What noun are you today?
- What game are you today?

What you will notice is suddenly you have an answer you couldn't have predicted. You will have a real insight into how they actually are AND you will have a meaningful engaging interaction with that child. That's what I call a Beyoncé-style 'upgrade ya.'

Investment: Build connections with positive affirmations
Action: Personal notes

When I was in secondary school I liked to pretend that I didn't care about anything. I wanted to make it really clear to the world that I was super cool and above everything. Obviously, that was not the case. I was mainly scared. I remember when I was in Year 8 my secondary teacher gave me a note. I had a tricky year and the note said 'I really appreciate your ability to bounce back from anything.' Well, I got some Blu-Tack and I stuck it on my wall and that's where it stayed until I left that room some many years later. Ever since then I have thought so carefully about the notes and the words which I share with my children. I know they continue to echo well beyond them being in my classroom. Notes can take many forms! It might be a proud post, a parent postcard, a happy bookmark, a sticky note or a written note on the table! The key is, making it a habit. Making it part of your routine and culture. Because, the two minutes it takes you to write that note means the actual world to your children. I've seen children hold their note all day long, read it to themselves over and over again and run frantically towards their parent to show them! They matter.

Piggy bank 'Missed payments'

We can't talk about building relationships without talking about repairing relationships. The thing is, we are human. We are human above everything else. Believe it or not, we are human before we are educators. Being human means that we will make mistakes. We need to remember, we are outnumbered in the classroom! So try as we might, there will be some days where a child might not feel as seen or as valued as another. Or we might slip up with one of our connection-focused routines. We may even feel like we were a bit snappy on a particularly teacher tired day. None of these are game over. None of these things make you a bad teacher. But that is where our secret sixth connection investment comes in: repair. It is one of the most important things we can do for our relationships. When we repair we are quite literally acknowledging what has happened, maybe even apologising and suggesting a solution moving forward. It might sound like this:

```
Year 2, I am so sorry I haven't been here for a few days. I have
been so busy around school and I really missed you. Why don't
we go out to play a little earlier today?

Or

Riley, I am so sorry I didn't respond when your hand was up. I
wanted to get everyone on the task. I am sorry if you felt like
I was ignoring you. Let's talk about it. What did you want to
tell me?
```

Piggy bank Shares

Wow! In all honesty I didn't realise I had this much financial terminology in my head but hey let's roll with it. Relationships go beyond interactions. You know that feeling when you're in a staff meeting or a training and your line leader shouts you out. You're recognised for an idea or you are asked for input. Your voice matters. How does it feel? Yes you are damn right, it feels great. Well we can do that for our children. We can make them feel valued for who they are and what they bring to the table. Here's how you can share that connection capital in your classroom.

Share the wealth: Child-centred planning and ideas

It's unlikely your children are going to be able to dictate your long-term planning – unless you're in a super progressive school in which case hit me up because I want to work with you. But there are always ways to include children in planning. For example, if you are doing traditional tales, show children a selection and get them to vote on which one they want next. Next time you're doing writing, let children choose which genre they want to write in. Ask children which scientist they want to learn more about. Put them in the driving seat.

Share the wealth: Child-centred routines

How are your children involved in setting routines and talking about the classroom? Is there a feedback box? Are there opportunities to discuss how they would like the next table layout or what class plant you should get?

Share the wealth: Pupil shout-outs

Simply that. Who have they noticed and why? Give your children opportunities to make deposits. It will support your class community as well as developing priceless collaboration skills.

Foster Formula

I realise that this chapter is a lot of information. What was really important to me when writing this chapter is that I'm not just giving you ideas or possibilities, I wanted to break it down to show you everything that I've learnt and practically what this looks like. Here is a Foster Formula I think is the perfect way to end this chapter.

Connection
before
correction.

TAKEAWAY BAG

- Connection is the most influential factor in achieving overall success and happiness.
- We can build in connection-based activities every day.
- We can develop a connection-focused culture.
- It's not about getting it right all of the time, it's about being human.

LIGHTS, CAMERA, ACTION REFLECTION

LIGHTS

What stood out to you in this chapter?

CAMERA

What does this look like for you right now? Tomorrow?

ACTION REFLECTION

What do you want to learn more about? What do you want to develop further?

CHAPTER 4

Behaviour and emotions

They are not giving you a hard time, they are having a hard time.

In this chapter we are opening up that emotions vault people! I'm sharing everything I have learnt about how developing our understanding of emotions is fundamental to supporting our pupils … WELL BEYOND them being in your classroom. I was lucky enough to interview Dr Emma Hepburn for this chapter and am very grateful for her insight.

'Where the hell did that come from?'

'Honestly, it was so random.'

'There was no reason for that behaviour.'

'What was that all about?'

Have you ever said any of those things about behaviour? I know I have! Dr Emma Hepburn, who is a psychologist and best-selling author of *A Toolkit For Your Emotions: 45 Ways To Feel Better*, said it best when she said:

Behaviour and emotions are intrinsically linked.

How we feel is fundamental to what we **do**. Emotions can help us make sense of many behaviours. I want to share with you three visuals to help us illustrate this. I think these visuals are a great way to enter this chapter and centre our mindset around the power of emotions. Side note: These are analogies to develop our understanding rather than direct representations of the brain.

The boiling pot

First up is the 'behaviour boiling pot'. I like this concept because it helps me to understand the fact that even though something is not visible yet it is still very much simmering away.

I mean, think about when your partner has said something you disagree with or didn't sit well with you. Often, we like to just keep that in the pot don't we? Then a few more things are said, it may be over the day or weeks even and BOOM, we're raging! For our partner, it is such a surprise, where did this come from? We've had a lovely day. But alas, there were feelings bubbling away there that just got a bit too big. This is the same for our children, but (naturally) they are developing their skillset to manage and understand those feelings. This means their boiling point is generally a bit quicker than ours!

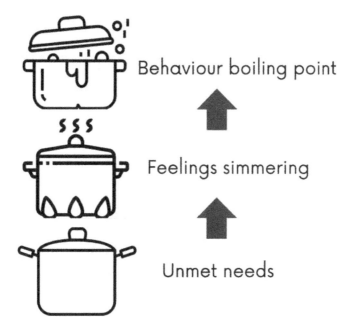

Dr Emma Hepburn highlights a key point about emotions that really aligns with this analogy. Trying to suppress emotions or pretend they aren't there is **cognitively demanding**. If our children don't have opportunities to notice how they feel or express their feelings safely, this can lead to more stress and you bet this will manifest into behaviour too!

The volcano

Now let's shimmy over to the behaviour volcano. I think this concept is really helpful when thinking about how behaviour can catch us by surprise. I mean, there are so many times in school where I have just been taken aback by behaviour. It can be so easy and convenient to go down the narrative that the behaviour was completely unprovoked and an isolated incident. But the reality is, that narrative is super unhelpful. If we see behaviour as **just behaviour** there are no solutions, no explanations and it is the child's issue. Taking us back to myth number 3 from Chapter 1. It can be easy for behaviour to just be expected and assumed based on previous experiences.

Oh, yeah they normally just walk out if they don't want to do it.

This can be really harmful for both you and the child. It sparks a negative cycle that just continues throughout their entire school life. Behaviour – consequence – behaviour – consequence. For you, have you ever felt like you were teaching on eggshells? Have you ever been teaching and just WAITING for a behaviour to erupt? I have, and the emotional burden and level of anxiety is strenuous. Using the volcano model we can ignite a different narrative. One where children and teachers are supported. Now that is a storyline I can get on board with! Another key aspect of this visual is we often see behaviour (and feelings) as completely irrational. But actually, they aren't. They are rational and valid for that child. Understanding that root, and that cause, *that* is how we support our children. Assuming and expecting the same responses from everyone? No one wins that game.

The body

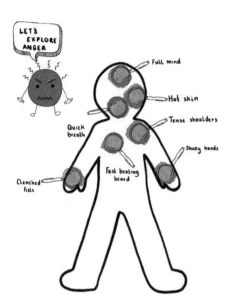

Our body provides data for how we feel. As Dr Emma Hepburn says, 'Our emotions are a description of how we feel physically and the context of what to do it with it' (Hepburn 2023). Our bodily sensations are an important part of the conversation because they develop understanding and expression of emotions. A child may not know they are feeling angry but they *can* feel their heart beating faster. It works the same way for us. We may not be able to say we are exhausted yet, but we *can* feel that headache. If we are trying to understand emotions better in the classroom, the body needs to be part of that learning. But don't fall into the trap that we all have exactly the same data! I know it seems like an *Alice in Wonderland* riddle (and in many ways it is) but what is key to know is that we don't need to be able to answer this riddle for every child. The goal isn't a perfect score sheet of every child's behaviour. We just need to be aware that there is more than meets the eye at play here. The goal is an updated equation of what behaviour is!

Let's put these models in action. You know what that means my friend? It is time to get our reflection on. First, let's have a little think about our own behaviour. There is absolutely no point trying to support children's behaviour if we have no awareness of our own. I want you to think about a time you behaved in a way you weren't proud of. It doesn't have to be anything wildly dramatic, just something that wasn't you at your best. I'll go first. I was in the car the other day with my husband on the way back from a family date and I was snapping at him. Short answers or no answers was my rule! I felt my irritation but I knew he hadn't actually done anything. Using these models let's unpick this further. I was definitely irritated and when I looked at it further I felt a bit exhausted. It had been a busy weekend and it was nearly over. What did I need? Quiet. That's just me. I need a balance of quiet, social and family in my life and when one is out I feel 'off' and stressed about how I am going to regain balance. So here, we have a helpful line of dialogue. Remember our Foster Formula? Curious over Furious. *When we ask questions, we can stop negative cycles. YOUR TURN!*

EXERCISE #4.1:

_____

_____

_____

_____

_____

_____

_____

_____

When you fill in the Exercise 4.1 box on the previous page have a think about the following questions:

- *What was your behaviour?*
- *What were you feeling?*
- *What did you need?*
- *How did your body feel?*

| SCRIPT SNIP |

If we know behaviour is coming from emotions, we can lead the conversation with that.

Rather than:
'What did you do?' or 'Why did you do that?'

Try:
'How are you feeling right now?'

Let's take it to the classroom

Children were doing a writing task. The calming music was on, everyone seemed focused and then a child said 'Ms Foster, Fion just scribbled on my work.' HUH? I came over to see that yes indeed, this boy had just scribbled all over her writing. Her 'big write' that she had worked so hard on. Deep breaths Jen. Get curious. Take and breath and then …

'Fion, what were you feeling when you did that?' Nothing. Hold the pause.

And then *'… Jealous'.* Breakthrough.

Fion was feeling jealous because he had low self-esteem in writing. That doesn't mean it makes it ok. But what it does mean, is we are able to separate the child from the behaviour. And that is a very powerful thing. That is when we can actually understand the feelings associated with behaviour and put an appropriate action and level of support in place. Note down your thoughts in the Exercise 4.2 box on the next page.

There isn't a Wikipedia flowchart of behaviours and feelings so it does require some investigative work with behaviour. Let's play a game. I will give you a behaviour and I want you to think about what feelings could have led to that behaviour.

A child sitting under a table.

EXERCISE #4.2:

_____

_____

_____

_____

_____

_____

_____

_____

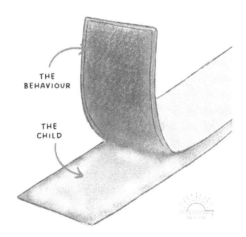

THE
BEHAVIOUR

THE
CHILD

Emotionsaurus

In order for us to really understand and support emotions in the classroom. We need to get our head around some of the emotional lingo!

Emotional intelligence

Research is always changing and adapting but let's simplify what we know now and why it's important. The term 'emotional intelligence' (Goleman 2020) refers to a person's overall ability to manage their emotions. Think of emotional intelligence as academic intelligence. It's the ultimate goal we want for our children. It is something we can grow for our children but we also need to be mindful that children will have different starting points and challenges.

Many people argue that emotional intelligence is more important than academic intelligence (Goleman 2020). Ooooh I know! But when you think about a time you really struggled with a task, is it because you weren't competent? Or was it because you had personal struggles? Your self-esteem was low? Was it to do with the actual task or was there another obstacle at play?

Think about the last big success you had. How much of it was your intellect? Or was it more about your resilience and how you managed unexpected hurdles? Or perhaps how you collaborated with others or stopped and looked after yourself when you needed a break? Something to mull over with your next cuppa!

Emotional literacy

Emotional literacy suggests a person's ability to communicate their emotions through words and read them in others (Gilbert et al. 2021). I like to think of it as the building block to emotional intelligence. The skills we can teach our children that build into their overall EQ.

If a child cannot communicate how they are feeling and what their needs are, their potential is completely stunted. Let's think back to our volcano or behaviour pot; if a child cannot communicate their feelings, what are we likely to see in terms of behaviour? If we don't give children the tools to identify what they are feeling, communicate it and have an idea of how to support themselves, they are likely to find themselves within a negative cycle.

Emotionally literate children are more successful. Period.

Picture a child you have known at school; they don't necessarily have to be a child you have taught but they have a reputation in the school. You know what kind of reputation I mean. Now tell me, without focusing on the behaviour, how emotionally literate was/is that child? *Are you having a lightbulb moment? Write their name down here, we can think about some support for them later in the chapter.*

UNPICKING WHAT BEHAVIOUR ACTUALLY IS

Regulation

Being regulated is when you are in a position when you are in control of your emotions and managing them. It doesn't necessarily mean you are fully calm and happy but it means your feelings are not taking over your thoughts and body. We all have the capacity to handle 'so much' before we feel like we lose control. Daniel Seigel calls this our 'window of tolerance' (Payne Bryson and Siegal 2012).

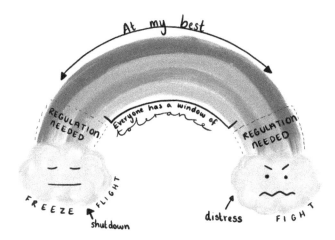

For example, let's say you are on the way to work in the car and you have caught two red lights in a row. You might feel a little disgruntled, but you're still in control. You might take a breath, put some music on and respond to what you need at that moment. Now let's say you get to work, someone has taken your parking space and then maybe when you finally find a space, you accidentally hit a pole. *Ok, we are now firmly out of the regulated zone. Write what your response would be below …*

UNPICKING WHAT BEHAVIOUR ACTUALLY IS

_____

_____

_____

_____

_____

_____

_____

_____

Dysregulated

Mine would be crying. Which leads me on to dysregulation. Dysregulation is when our feelings overpower our ability to manage them. I don't care if I'm late now. I don't care who sees. I'm crying. I can't stop it. When we are dysregulated, our brain and bodies function in our stress responses. So how do we support a dysregulated child (or adult for that matter!)?

Co-regulation

This is simply the process of sharing your calm. Being that calm anchor for a child. It might be breathing with them, modelling calming strategies or simply just being there as a calm presence. Imagine you are feeling dysregulated right, do you want your best friend or partner to offer advice at this point? Not really. Do you want to talk through what happened? Not so much. Mainly, you just want to know that they are *there*. Sharing their calm rather than creating further chaos.

Self-regulation

Something you and I have developed over time. We have learnt to take slow breaths, go outside, lay down or respond to what our body needs. Children haven't. The only way they can learn self-regulation is through a co-regulation pit stop and being explicitly taught the skills.

Mindfulness

As you read this, wiggle your toes. Feel the way they push against your shoes, and the weight of your feet on the floor. Really think about what your feet feel like right now – their heaviness. Being mindful, literally means being completely present and aware in the moment. You just did a mini mindfulness meditation.

MRI scans show that engaging in mindfulness activities regularly over an eight-week period has an impact on how our brain responds and activates (Powell 2018). Especially, during moments of overwhelm.

Imagine giving children the tools to tackle those tough moments with confidence!

Let's talk about Jaden

I was out of class one morning and heard screams in another class. I came in to find two children in a physical altercation. The teacher was standing in the middle of them trying to stop it. Jaden had a pen in his hand very close to pushing into the teacher. His eyes were darting and his breathing was uneven. Jaden was dysregulated. Let's think, what would not work here?

- Threatening him with consequences (that will only escalate this feeling).
- Giving him choices (they will not be heard).
- Using force (the adrenaline in him is probably sky high).

So what does that leave us with? Sharing our calm. Co-regulation. I didn't know what was going to happen, but for me, this was the only choice. And just to clarify here, I am not recommending teachers put themselves in dangerous positions. I am simply sharing this for context. I walked in and I touched him calmly on the shoulders and looked him in the eye. 'It is ok. I am here. I've got you. I've got you. I've got you.' He softened. I was able to take the pen and move him out of the room calmly.

It seems radical but think about yourself back in that car park scenario. Imagine your boss coming to shout at you because you are going to be late or receiving an ultimatum to choose from. What if someone tried dragging you out? None of these options make me feel safe to be honest! How about, a co-worker comes and sits in the seat next to you. They just sit there and after a while say, 'It's ok, I'm here.' Ahhh that's nice isnt it? Like a sip of hot chocolate on a cold day. That is the power of co-regulation!

Now what I want to do is ensure Jaden doesn't reach a point where he is in danger or putting others in danger. But now is not the time to say 'deep breath in ...' Because that is incredibly infuriating. Which leads me to my next point.

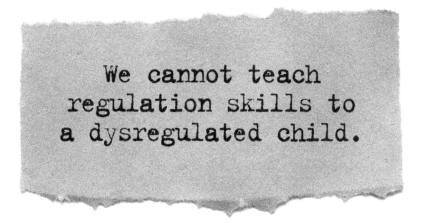

We cannot teach regulation skills to a dysregulated child.

It must be taught BEFORE. But where on earth do we start? For me, I find systematic approaches helpful because we are all using the same framework, language and understanding. That's why I like Claude Steiner's emotional awareness scale which is an amazing tool (Steiner 2003). As educators, we can use this to assess children and plan for emotional literacy systematically.

100% awareness

Interactivity
Knowing how to support and respond to others
when they are experiencing certain emotions

Empathy
The ability to feel what others around
us are feeling and being sensitive to it

Causality
Understanding the cause behind emotions

Differentiation
Being able to recognise differences in emotions like anger or
jealousy. Also understanding that all emotions are spectrums
and can be felt with a range of different intensities.

Verbal barrier
An important stage in the transition from Low to high
emotional awareness. Requires the use of our pre-frontal cortex,
responsible for language, thinking and rationalising to be able to
express what we feel and why.

Most of our students will be at this stage

Primal experience
Person is conscious of emotions but cannot name them
or communicate them. (Similar to babies.)

Some children
with trauma
may be here

Physical sensations
When emotions cannot be cognitively comprehended they are experienced
and communicated through bodily responses. For example. Extreme fatigue
closely correlates with depression

Numbness
Person not aware of any states they feel, even when
undergoing intense emotions

0% awareness

I think this visual is helpful when we are thinking about support over punishment. Too often behaviour leads to consequences and judgement. This visual helps me remember, ok, what can the child actually do and what do they need my help with? Take Jaden for example. Jaden was somewhere between Primal experience and Verbal barrier. Jaden, who had unfairly experienced trauma was unable to identify these feelings. Jaden had a smaller window of tolerance and was unable to identify and communicate his feelings before he experienced dysregulation. Remember that child's name you wrote down? Where do you think they would be on the scale? What do you think they would benefit from?

In the box on the next page, consider these two things:

- *On the scale they would be:*
- *I think they would benefit from:*

Now remember, we cannot teach a child regulation skills when they are dysregulated. Remember the last person to tell you to 'Calm down' when you were losing it? How did that go down? Our brains just are not able to comprehend a learning process while we are experiencing high levels of stress. So, what can we do when children are regulated to support them in those moments?

UNPICKING WHAT BEHAVIOUR ACTUALLY IS

_____
_____
_____
_____
_____
_____
_____
_____

Emotional tool: Check-ins

With all the questions we ask on a daily (if not hourly) basis, how many are linked to our children's wellbeing? And if we are saying 'How are you?' how much time do we really give for it? Have you ever been asked 'How are you?' and said 'fine' within a heartbeat? Or 'Good, how are you?' as an instinctual response? Have you ever said it when you actually were not fine? How did that day pan out for you? Were you snappy? Did you bubble over? Did it get worse? Why didn't we answer truthfully? Is it because we felt the person didn't genuinely care about the response? Was it more small talk than real talk? Did we not have enough time? When we make time to explore, validate and support our students' emotions, we are providing our pupils with the highest possible support and opportunity. This is a great example of using daily connection coins because we are showing a genuine interest in our children.

Imagine the new heights our children could reach if we nurture who they are as a person before we tackle who they are as a learner! A check-in is quite literally a way to see how children are feeling emotionally. Children tell you how they are currently feeling using a method of your choice. Here are some ideas:

- having children circle the emotion they are feeling. This could be a desk check-in;
- having children peg their name or face to the emotion they are feeling;

- using a digital check-in like Google Forms;
- informally asking children in the register;
- using journals for children to personally check-in.

Why the check-in is so valuable

I first started doing a check-in in Year 1. Children put lolly sticks into cups with emotions on and suddenly, I had this data. I had this insider information about the children in my class before I had even done the register. What this meant is I could then ask children privately about their feelings now that I had an opening lead. Here was the magic, I could then provide the support they needed for that emotion to be validated and their needs to be met. What did this mean? That behaviour pot never boiled. The volcano didn't erupt. Because I could intervene. I could identify the problem and work with the child to find a solution because a feeling felt by yourself can be very overwhelming. Maybe it was a peer conflict, maybe they weren't sure if they had their lunchbox or maybe it was a bad sleep. But either way ... VALUABLE data I never would have known without that check-in.

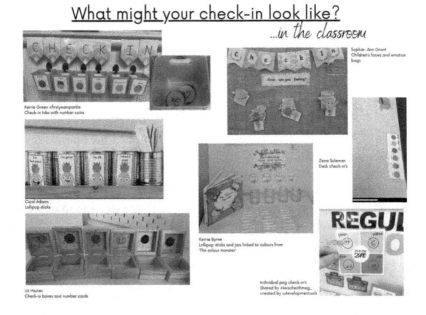

What might your check-in look like?
...in the classroom

Emotional tool: Emotional literacy books

You know, when I was growing up I don't remember so many beautiful books about feelings. Picture books are amazing tools to support children to visualise concepts they don't fully understand yet. Matt Haig put it beautifully when he said: 'Through fiction you can escape into a world that isn't your life, but can help you to deal with it' (Guest 2017). I liked that. I think when you are talking about 'characters' instead of yourself, it feels a lot safer doesn't it? Any picture book (or book for that matter) can support emotional literacy as long as we construct our questions that way:

- How do you think the character was feeling here?
- Do you think the character felt just one feeling?
- What other choice do you think the character could have made?
- Would you feel the same if it was you?

For younger children you can use tools such as an emotion octopus, feeling cards or feeling puppets to support their understanding. For specific books on emotions check out The Emotions Shelf (www.goodmorningmsfoster.com/theemotionsshelf).

Emotion tool: Modelling

Probably one of the most effective things we can do. Regular modelling from trusted adults supports children to feel safe in their understanding and develop their confidence with communicating (Gilbert et al. 2021). It also provides children with answers they may have been too nervous to acquire through a live example. That's why it works so well when we have 'made a mistake' in class and they get to be the teacher. It is that feeling again of seeing someone else experience and work through it. It feels safer than it being you! This might sound like:

SCRIPT SNIP

I am feeling a bit annoyed because the photocopier is broken! It is annoying because I hadn't expected it to happen and now I have to rethink what I wanted to do with you this lesson. I am going to take some breaths and come up with a plan once my head is clear. Do you want to do it with me? Shall we do bumble bee breathing?

   Or

I am feeling a bit tired today. I didn't sleep very well. Have you ever not slept well? It is making it hard for me to focus. I wonder what I could do to feel a bit better?

Mirroring demonstrates how we imitate the behaviours of those who we spend the most time with (Gilbert et al. 2021). So basically, we are teaching all the time. We are modelling all the time. Children will be observing and processing how we express and regulate our emotions. So these examples really are super powerful ways to support our children.

Emotional tool: Emotional vaccines

Coined by Dr Becky Kennedy (Kennedy 2022) this really is revolutionary. The concept of emotional vaccines is talking through and supporting a child (or children) about something that might be overwhelming ... before it happens. For example, let's say you have a fire drill. Children are likely to feel unsettled and some may even feel triggered and distressed. The week of the fire drill you might say something like:

> My loves, there is going to be a fire drill this week. That means it is a practice. It isn't real. Even though it is not real it might feel like a bit of a shock? What else might we feel? We might find it too loud? Hmm I wonder what we could do to support ourselves if we find it too loud?

Here what we are doing is having an open discussion and preparing for it. Often the shock of a feeling is what is most triggering. Why am I so unsettled? I didn't expect to be so confused? It is the surprise that really hits us. If we remove the shock with an emotional vaccine, we can then really focus on strategies.

Emotion tool: Breathing

Oh you know, only the most important thing we can do EVER. Breathing is so crazy powerful like I didn't even realise until I was pregnant! Here is what I wish I knew. Read it once and then do it with me.

> Inhale for four seconds, pause for four seconds, exhale for four seconds.

Go on, do it again. I like to use my fingers to count up and down in fours. It feels great right? It is one of those most amazing tools at our disposal that supports us to regulate. Mmmm but my children won't engage with 'breathing'. I HEAR YOU. I worried about this too. But there are so many ways to engage with breathing like drawing, moving, watching. What if you watched a guided video? What if you did balancing and breathing? Or what if you drew your breath? What if you used a tool like a breathing board or squeezy ball? This skill is too important to let it not be taught. There is always a way!

PS Just a disclaimer ...

I wouldn't recommend asking young children to hold their breath for four seconds. I would start by just mindfully inhaling through the nose and exhaling through the mouth. That in itself is a challenge if you've never been exposed to it!

Emotions and time out

Time out is when a child is asked to sit away from you or the other children because of their behaviour. Have I done it before? Yes, I have. But, when we know better, we do better! We will explore time out in Chapter 9, Behaviour and consequences, but let's think about it from an emotional perspective. What's the problem?

- It tells children that their feelings are uncomfortable to be around.
- We are making children feel like they are bad and their big feelings should be suppressed.
- We are telling children we don't care about their feelings and we don't want to see them.

When children are dysregulated the last thing they need is isolation. They need safety. They need an anchor. They need to know that they are accepted for who they are and will be supported. This doesn't mean allowing dangerous behaviours, I am aware that these happen and the safety of you and your students is THE utmost priority. But focusing on the feelings supports us to meet those needs before their emotions hit that boiling pot. It enables us to develop a culture of empathy and curiosity where we can actually stop negative cycles of behaviour.

The emotion myths

There are negative and positive emotions Sometimes we don't even mean to send this message. I mean I am guilty of saying 'don't cry'. But when we categorise emotions as negative and positive we accidentally lace a layer of shame on top. Children don't want to feel certain emotions because it might displease you. They might be ashamed or embarrassed about certain emotions and think that they themselves are not good. I like to talk about emotions as being comfortable and uncomfortable because that is how we feel them. We can also talk about emotions as having high or low energy which helps our understanding of them. I think it is helpful to talk about them as passing visitors. They come and they go and they are telling us something about ourselves.

Imagine a world where you were never angry or never cried. We want to feel. We want our children to be passionate, loving and expressive. We don't want to stop emotions, we just want to support children to understand and manage them. Rather than saying 'There is no reason to be angry.' We might say 'Hmm tell me more about what is making you angry and we can work together to resolve it.'

Emotions have the same packaging

There are a lot of assumptions and expectations around emotions and behaviour. But one thing we need to remember is that how we respond to a situation is not the same as the person sitting next to us, or opposite us. But all of them are valid. Emotions are unique to individuals; removing our assumptions allows us to really support our children when they need it most.

Emotions are not irrational

Dr Emma Hepburn does an amazing job of combatting this stereotype (Hepburn 2023). Emma tells us emotions are informed, not rational. They share data about your body and brain at a given time and that is important and should be recognised as such.

The last message I want to leave you with is:

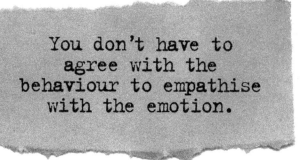

You don't have to agree with the behaviour to empathise with the emotion.

TAKEAWAY BAG

- Emotions are an important factor in understanding behaviour.
- We can build children's emotional intelligence.
- We can use everyday tools to proactively support children's wellbeing.

LIGHTS, CAMERA, ACTION REFLECTION

LIGHTS

What stood out to you in this chapter?

CAMERA

What does this look like for you right now? Tomorrow?

ACTION REFLECTION

What do you want to learn more about? What do you want to develop further?

CHAPTER 5

Behaviour and the classroom

I remember the first time I stepped foot into my first classroom. All mine baby, all mine. You kind of feel like you're a homeowner, or a monarch, either way, it is a great vibe. This was very quickly followed by sheer panic. What in the love of coffee was I supposed to do with a classroom anyway? What do you mean I need to set it up? By myself? No one ever told me. Does it not come ready made? Oh, and do I have to like, buy stuff? Where do I begin? I actually went into my classroom every day for a week. A week. Do you want to know what I did? Well the majority of the time I swivelled on my chair pretending I was Dr Evil tbh. The rest of the time? Googling what I should do and pretending I knew. A trés boring game. I wouldn't recommend it.

But why does this matter? I thought this was a book about behaviour? Well, your class will spend an estimated 1,170 hours at school. During term time, they will spend the majority of their life at school. They will spend most of that time in your classroom. Think about how annoying it is when something in your house is untidy, broken, not serving a purpose, uncomfortable etc. We have the power as grown ass adults to fix it. To curate a space that makes us happy and benefits us. Our children do not have that. Imagine sitting at a wobbly table for six weeks or never being able to fully see the board because of the glare. Or hitting another chair every time you pull yours out? Classrooms matter. And they most definitely are a key factor when talking about behaviour in schools.

Now that we all agree classrooms matter you are probably starting to whizz through your archives of classrooms or maybe you're just having a moment of silence to feel as clueless as I was. WELL, let me save you the emotional burden my friend. I thought it would be fun to share some of my clueless classroom moments over the years and all have a little giggle. Stay tuned because in this chapter we will be breaking down what you ACTUALLY need to know about classrooms and behaviour.

But first, Jen Foster. This is your life:

2012

My classroom displays were mainly wallpaper. Heavily laminated (can you be heavily laminated?). I didn't refer to them and the children didn't either. When I say 'point', you say 'less'. Point …

2013

I discovered the world of DaFont. A website with downloadable fonts. Imagine a font explosion and then add random colours to that. Yeah. Swirly fonts, patterned fonts, bubble fonts, I wanted them all! However, no one could read them. Some actually made our eyes hurt! Imagine that? Imagine how that might then impact behaviour.

2016

I started looking at a needs-focused classroom. This was also the first year I started leading behaviour. Great intentions and the right track was there … somewhere. But I just bought a bunch of things that I didn't explain to the children. Personal lockers, soft furnishings, tools for regulation etc. It ended up unused or misused. I distinctly remember a teacher saying to me, 'Why do you bother? They don't deserve it.' It made me so angry but I was pretty lost as I couldn't see it working.

2017

I fell. I fell down the Pinterest hole. I had rainbows, bright colours everywhere, random quotes in swirly writing, FEATHER BOA BORDERS. For crying out loud Jen you hot mess. How much of it actually supported my children? How much of it hindered their learning or wellbeing? Head in hands.

2021

My first, truly child-led/research-based classroom. It was our home. During end-of-year discussions a child said to me: 'I am just really going to miss this classroom, I have never had one like this before and I don't think I ever will again. I love it here.'

Did you enjoy that? Ok, your turn. Have a think about something in your classroom that was just not purposeful. If you haven't had a classroom yet, have a think about something you have seen. In the box below, have a think about: *What did you see? Why was it not purposeful? Did it help learning, behaviour or wellbeing or did it actively hinder learning, behaviour or wellbeing?*

UNPICKING WHAT BEHAVIOUR ACTUALLY IS

_____

_____

_____

_____

_____

_____

_____

I'm bringing 'BAE' back

So where do we start? How can we achieve a classroom that ACTIVELY supports behaviour in our class?

Do you remember when everyone used to say BAE? What happened to that? ANYWHO, we are going to use this to help us break down our needs-focused classroom.

BAE classrooms encompass:

B – Basic needs

A – Academic needs

E – Emotional needs

B for Basic needs

Have you ever been sitting in staff training in total discomfort? I mean, who hasn't? Let's be real. But journey back to that feeling. I remember sitting on the dinner hall tables during a twilight. No back support? I mean, I am not that old but I will tell you right now, I _am_ unfit and my back can't handle that madness for two hours. I also remember sitting on one of those child chairs for a two-hour training session while seven months pregnant. I'll tell you right now, I wasn't listening to a damn thing. _Have a think about a time your basic needs weren't met and how it impacted you and your behaviour ... jot down your thoughts in the box below._

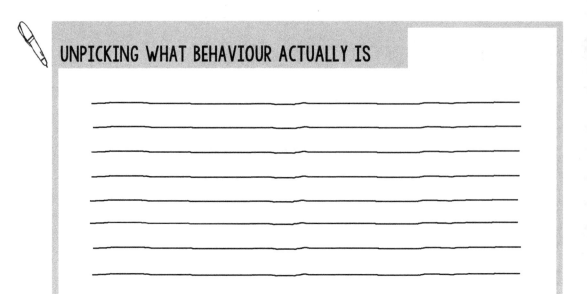

UNPICKING WHAT BEHAVIOUR ACTUALLY IS

What Khan taught me

When it comes to basic needs it is often one of those aspects that gets missed off the list. It falls behind aesthetics and sorting our teacher desk. But as you PROBS guessed from the name. *Basic* needs are the utmost priority in the classroom. If these are not met you WILL see it in behaviour. One of my most resounding examples of this happened when I was teaching Year 1. We were coming to the end of a writing lesson and I noticed a child hadn't written a single thing. Ignoring my instinctual irritation I said 'Khan, you haven't written anything. Are you ok? That is not like you.' To which he answered: 'The air con is on above me and I am really cold.' Instant embarrassment at that initial irritation I suppressed. That could have been a whole other story if I reacted differently and on another day, I might have. But as we know, the behaviour is not the child. It is our job to meet those needs before they manifest into behaviours. So what are those basic needs we need to consider? Here is a checklist I now use when I am setting up a classroom (and you can download this to use too!).

Let's break these down a bit further shall we:

Every child has a chair

Seems basic but all my class teachers out there will know, sometimes this is not the case. I would also add that the chair should be at the right height. The same way we don't want to sit on a miniature chair, our children should have that same comfort right?

Every child can see the board

I mean, classrooms are wild spaces. They aren't built like cinemas! I would recommend just sitting in every chair and experiencing what that chair feels like for a child. Once, I realised my washing line display was dangling dangerously low by a child's chair!

Can children move comfortably?

Pull out the chair. Does it hit a wall? Another chair? A table? Can you imagine how annoying that would be every lesson! Definitely worth moving around a bit!

Do children have a carpet space?/Carpet organisation

Is Tommy too squashed? Is Gina too close to the front? Children are on the carpet so often, let's make sure they have a space that is suitable.

Accommodations for neurodivergent pupils

If you have a child in your class who is neurodivergent it is important their needs are met as soon as they enter your class. It might be that they wear noise-cancelling headphones, have a wobble cushion or a gym band on their chair. Double check with your SENCo as they will have that information.

Name labels/Belongings organised

I remember my Year 4 class coming upstairs on my first day teaching. As they went to the coat hooks there was this confused/distressed murmuring ... I forgot/didn't realise I needed to have name labels there. At the time this seemed pretty minor but now I know the impact of a name label. Belonging. A sense of belonging is so important, especially in those first few weeks. So yeah, labels would have helped make that connection straight away and ensure children felt settled.

Equipment organisation/Book organisation

This will limit the amount of unsettled behaviour in your classroom. Fact. No snatching for that last pencil. No 'faff' when all of the systems rely on you and you're on your last legs! Child-led, well-oiled systems mean you spend less time stressing and more time teaching. What do I mean by this? All children have the equipment they need, there is enough for every child and this is easily accessible. This looks different for every teacher and classroom but those are the principles. And books? Children know where their books are, children can hand out and collect books easily, that is about it! Easier said than done I know. For these systems, they aren't ready made and delivered unfortunately. They do take time to get the right one! A bit of a Goldilocks vibe. So be ready to trial and trash systems where needed. Every class is different.

A note

This isn't a list of unrealistic actions. If we don't have these in our classrooms our senior leaders must make it happen. Period. In the same breath, most of these are out of your control. Please don't go online and buy a set of classroom chairs! If you feel like the basic needs are not being met in your classroom, talk to your senior leaders and be honest with your children. I once didn't have the right number of tables for five weeks! I just had to make do with what I could scavenge in my school! I apologised to my children but let them know I was working on it. Because I knew the tables weren't right, I increased my carpet time as all children were comfortable there. I changed my lesson format to align this. The point is, do what you can with what you have.

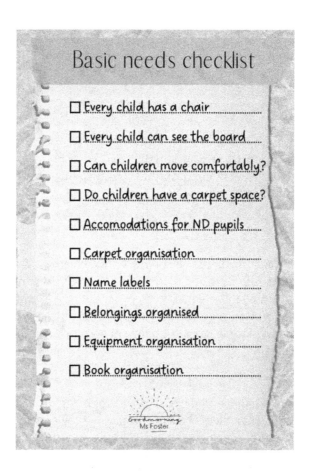

A is for Academic needs

Here's the thing. Behaviour is often put into a box and dealt with separately. But it isn't separate at all. When we put it all together and focus on what that child needs to succeed and flourish … we can make easier choices that have a great impact for our children.

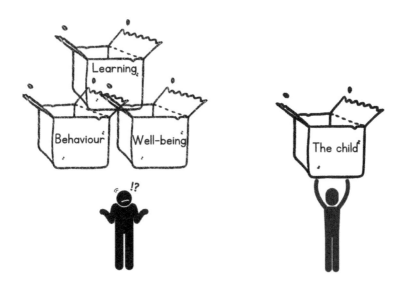

What Marco taught me

In my first year of teaching I had a child in my class who hated being there. Marco made it very known. He would attend different phonics and maths groups in the morning but every afternoon he was with me. He would make noises, crawl under the table and answer back. I thought it was just good old-fashioned 'defiance'. However, it turned out he couldn't access my lessons. He could barely read (in Year 4) and had a horrible case of low self-esteem. Once I realised this, I thought about how suffocating it must have felt to be in a class where you were just so agonisingly confused. Now, this isn't a section about learning in particular (that will come later) but I realised I could make adjustments in my classroom to support the academic needs of all my pupils. This is by no means an exhaustive list. Hell, this could be a book in itself. But these are just some small changes (classroom specific) that made a world of difference. And by the way, Marco? Became one of my loved pupils, making remarkable progress in more ways than one.

Visuals

Marco taught me to be mindful of how much text I was using in the classroom. Was it all needed? Was it an information overload? If it was for the children, how helpful was it? I limited my text in displays way down and invested in visuals more. The way we communicate through visuals is super speedy and universal. It made my classroom that much more accessible.

Fonts

Bye Bye DaFont. We had some fun didn't we? HA! Ok we don't need to cancel DaFont, but we do need to be mindful of whether children can actually read the fonts we are using on displays. Because if they can't? What is the point?

Clutter

I personally cannot learn if there is clutter. That's just me. But I know I can't be the ONLY one. Clutter can add unnecessary barriers to learning and, in this job, we don't need any more barriers!

Support

So let's say I was confused in the task, what would I do? John Hattie talks about teachers seeing learning through the eyes of students and helping them become their own teachers. So how can we do this in the classroom? Have aids for children that they can freely get. This might be a word bank area, dictionaries, sentence starter zone, communication and print resources, cubes, number lines, numicon. I COULD GO ON and probably bore you to death. Basically, how can they complete the task without you? Put support in your room and make it clear that children can get this when they need it!

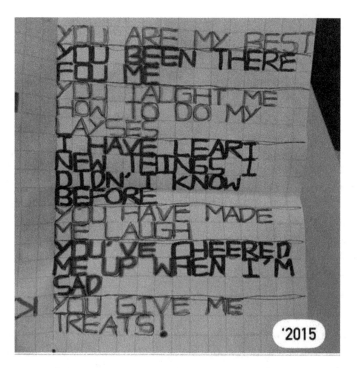

A note from Marco

E is for Emotional needs

Let me paint a picture for you. Your alarm doesn't go off, you spill hot coffee on yourself on the way to school (where there is a crazy amount of traffic). When you get in (late), you cannot turn your computer on. What do you do? Do you throw a chair? Do you scream? Do you leave the building? No. These options are generally frowned upon in the adult world. We self-regulate. We breathe, we put some music on, we talk to someone, we maybe even have a cry in the toilet but my point is we have strategies that we know will make us feel better. We use these strategies and we adapt. Yet, many classrooms don't do the same for our kids.

Let's reverse the scenario. A child – let's call her Chloe. Has a bad sleep, her milk was off in her breakfast, when she gets to school, someone is sitting in her carpet spot. When she tries to tell the teacher, the teacher tells her to stop talking. Another child laughs at her. In her first lesson, her whiteboard pen isn't working. She can't find another one, now she is too scared to tell the teacher. The teacher then sees she has not written her words. 'Oh dear Chloe. Someone is a bit sleepy today. Hurry up, get your words down.' There are about three points in that scenario where Chloe needs to take some time, to self-regulate, to re-centre.

We are not giving our children the opportunity to be children, or human for that matter. This brings me to …

What Rudi taught me

I taught Rudi after the pandemic in Year 2. She was one of thousands of children who struggled with post-Covid symptoms both physical and emotional. This escalated quite uncontrollably and she became completely detached from school. She would come in crying and often cry for an hour or two. I want to share with you three features you can include in your classroom that can support every single child with the understandable emotional hurdles of everyday life: calm space, check-in and a visual timetable. Oh and Rudi? Talks about that time so eloquently and courageously and will forever go down as one of my most memorable and special pupils.

A calm space

A calm space is what it says on the tin. A space for regulation, restoration and rest. WE NEED THAT in our day. Our children do too. Without a calm space we leave our children alone with big feelings that will either explode or implode. Without a calm space, we might look at behaviour as 'misbehaviour' rather than dysregulation. We need to remember we are teaching individuals not just 'students' and we have to care for them both pastorally and academically. A calm space doesn't necessarily have to be a corner of your room. It just needs to be a provision children can access. It might be an area of the room if you are lucky enough to obtain one. But it could also just be a toolbox with calming strategies or even one single choosing board. It may be a desk outside your classroom or a tray children can access. The point is, there is always a way to support our children to access emotional support. BEWARE of the Pinterest Pop-Up Calm Space! Contrary to some corners of the internet, a calm space does not require seventeen laminated posters, drapes and mood lighting. It is simply a designated space for calm.

So what might go in a calm space?

It really depends on the needs of your children and there is definitely not a 'set list' but let's go back to that purpose. We want to create opportunities for regulation, rest and restorative support. Here are *some* ideas and don't worry I will break them down!

What might I have in a Calm Space?

Regulate	Rest	Repair
Breathing boards	Ear defenders	Restorative reflections
Play-dough	Colouring	Check-ins
Sensory tools/ Fidgets	Doodling	Feelings posters
Sensory timers	Reading	Choice board
Bubble wrap	Eye mask	

BREATHING BOARDS

As we learnt from Chapter 4, 'Behaviour and emotions', breathing is a big deal. But breathing can be kind of boring. That's why breathing tools are really helpful. This board from the Little Coach House (www.littlecoachhouse.co.uk/) supports children to regulate their breathing by incorporating both touch and a visual aid. Genius!

PLAY-DOUGH/SENSORY TOOLS AND BUBBLE WRAP

When you are able to manipulate a material with your hands, there is a sense of control. This is really effective when you're feeling dysregulated. The repeated motion is also very soothing. Busy hands support busy minds!

SENSORY TIMER

There is something so incredibly mesmerising about a sensory timer! It is a great way to find your calm. I would also recommend glitter jars!

EAR DEFENDERS AND EYE MASKS

For those times when you just need to block everything out. A classroom can feel like Trafalgar Square on New Year's Eve when you're dysregulated!

COLOURING/DOODLING/READING

It is totally child dependent but these activities can be super calming. I once just stuck down some adhesive whiteboard paper on my calm space table and this was constantly used for doodling.

RESTORATIVE CONVERSATIONS

A calm space is a great area for processing an incident. You can read more about this in Chapter 12, 'Behaviour and restorative practice'.

CHECK-INS/FEELINGS BOARDS

As we saw in Chapter 4, 'Behaviour and emotions', having a wellbeing check-in as part of your classroom means we have a very welcome 'middle man' between feelings and behaviour. When we can support a child to identify a feeling that is uncomfortable or overwhelming, we can intervene and meet those needs. Having feelings resources and a check-in is a really helpful addition to a calm space.

CHOICE BOARD

A great management tool for the calm space where a child can choose what they are going to do. It might look like this:

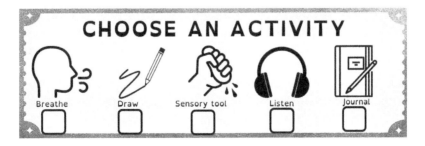

It's not working!

Before you create a calm space in your classroom, think really carefully about how you set it up. I have seen lots of educators print off a calm corner pack and stick it all up. Although, I understand the intentions are good, this is not helpful for your children. It is the equivalent to Jen circa 2012 sticking up a Place Value display and never referring to it. Don't be Jen 2012.

I hate to be the person to break it to you but you can't just set up a calm space and expect children to know what to do. It simply will not work and then you are back to square one. Cue, Jen 2016. You need to take the time to explore emotions as a class. Here are some (trialled and tested) steps to help your calm space be as successful as possible:

1. Before we 'launch' a calm space, children actually need to develop their emotional literacy (see Chapter 7) to fully understand why a calm space can be beneficial to their wellbeing and their time in the classroom.
2. I find picture books are the most incredible communicative tools for introducing unknown concepts. I would recommend using *Addie's Me Cave* by Rachael Ostrowski and Cheryl Palladino (2021). I also designed a short picture book to support my children. It is called *My Mind is Full* (you can access this in downloads).
3. 'Children have never been very good at listening to their elders, but they have never failed to imitate them' (Baldwin 1961). Modelling is one of the best tools we have in our toolbox. TALK about how you are feeling. Talk about your awful commute to work, the photocopier breaking down and what YOU did about it. Talk about how you supported yourself. Children look up to you. Give them something real.
4. Exploring calming tools (gradual and add gradually). I found that calm tools can be very exciting and mysterious so I normalised it. I created opportunities for all children to explore them and discuss how it made them feel. This way it wasn't a game. It was a lesson. If they are only allowed to use them once they are dysregulated, you will find a lot of children begin to 'feel dysregulated'. Take the novelty out of it and set up a carousel session where children can explore them all.
5. Agreement/Rule. Proactive over reactive. Take the time to talk to your children about how the calm space will work and agree on this together. I would recommend two to four agreed rules that children can remember. For example: we ask a teacher before entering, we always tidy up afterwards, we treat the calm space respectfully. Obviously, make it suitable for your children but keep it simple!
6. Calm pass. This can be handy to keep things explicit. I used a calm pass so children had to have one in order to access the calm space. It had the rules on it and just added that extra structure. I would give this to children so it worked as a kind of 'ticket' for entry.

Note
It won't be this super structured forever! It is just important to keep it simple and clear when you are first implementing it. By the end of the year it will look a lot more child led.

A check-in

We have explored check-ins in the previous chapter and we know having a wellbeing check-in as part of your classroom means we have a very welcome 'middle man' between feelings and behaviour. When we can support a child to identify a feeling that is uncomfortable or overwhelming, we can intervene and meet those needs.

What might this look like in your classroom?

There are so many ways to do a wellbeing check-in in your classroom but here are six ideas to get you thinking! The core principle is children have an opportunity to identify how they are feeling.

1. Named lollipop sticks/pegs and emotions baskets. Children can put their item in the feeling they are currently in.
2. Desk check-ins. Children can circle the feeling with a whiteboard pen.
3. Digital check-ins. If you are lucky enough to have a couple of devices, children can complete a morning Google form.
4. A Velcro board with numbers or faces. Children can move their number or face to the emotion.
5. Journals! Children can check-in personally in their journal each morning or after each transition. This could come from a journal prompt.
6. For autistic children, be mindful that the correlation between the language of emotions and sensation of emotions might not match up. I would recommend using Autism Level Up free resources (www.autismlevelup.com/#tools) to provide appropriate check-ins for all pupils.

Why must it be routinely?

Because we must never ever miss an opportunity to support our pupils! Just like we never miss a maths lesson (cough cough, ok – try not to) we do the same for our pastoral needs.

How might you follow up?

If a child has disclosed that they are feeling angry, sad or worried, it is important we are there for them as early as possible. Some of the things I have done is introducing a soft start. I may have an independent activity or a story playing so I can follow up. If you are lucky to have your TA in class, they can cover for a few minutes. I have also followed up at break time where I have found no other time. Nine times out of ten it is something you can fix right there on the spot. Some of the issues children have raised during check-in to me have been: I am worried that xx isn't my friend any more/I don't think my mum packed my school lunch/I didn't sleep well/I don't have my homework/I had a stone in my shoe/I am worried about the spelling test.

And so we close that classroom door and hopefully you are in a much better place than Jen circa 2012. A big thank you to the children in this chapter who taught me so much. So what is next for you and your classroom?

What is a visual timetable?

Have you ever showed up at a training day or a long meeting with no agenda? You might be worrying if you were supposed to prepare for something. You might be internally freaking out and externally tapping your pen! You might try and talk to a friend and figure out if they know anything. One thing is for sure, you won't be calm and focused. That is what our children experience every time they step into a classroom without a visual timetable. Honestly, I had no idea. I felt like it was just an extra job that I did not have time for. But when I started really investing time into updating my visual timetable I noticed something. Children were more settled at the beginning of the day and especially between lessons.

Top Tips!

1. Use clear visuals. If you use specific symbols in your school such as Widget (www. widgit.com/), then absolutely stay consistent with that. If you do not have access to a specific software I would suggest simple icons. You can find these using Flaticon (www.flaticon.com/) or Canva (www.canva.com/).

2. Share with children at the beginning of the day. Talk through each aspect and what they can expect.
3. If possible, share between lessons. This might just be taking an icon off. 'We have finished our reading for today now so let's remove that from the timetable, well done everyone.' This is a great hit of dopamine too!
4. If you have something out of the ordinary that day, share it. I used to add a sticky note to the timetable. This was a visual reminder for myself and the children.

My visual timetable was from a small business. This is absolutely not necessary. You can create your own or download versions online. This is just an example.

TAKEAWAY BAG

- Your classroom matters.
- Basic needs are the utmost priority.
- Functionality over aesthetics!
- We can support emotions within our classroom through calm spaces and check-ins.
- Every classroom should have a visual timetable.

LIGHTS, CAMERA, ACTION REFLECTION

LIGHTS

What stood out to you in this chapter?

CAMERA

What does this look like for you right now? Tomorrow?

ACTION REFLECTION

What do you want to learn more about? What do you want to develop further?

CHAPTER 6

Behaviour and rewards

In this chapter, we are switching that IPHONE 14 (or whatever it is now) torch light on rewards. I am spilling the peppermint tea on everything I wish I was told about rewards. By the end of this chapter you will be tearing down that whole-class reward system (or at least thinking about it differently). This chapter is about **whole-class** reward systems.

Before we move forward with this chapter I want to share 'the carrot and the stick' concept (Smith 2015). This is the idea that in order to make the donkey do the desired work you need to either incentivise action with the carrot or instil fear with the stick. This is rewards and consequences in its most basic form. I didn't hear this phrase until about my eighth year of teaching and the visual alone created such a trigger of thought and reflection for me. I wanted to start with this image to get us in the mindset of reflection.

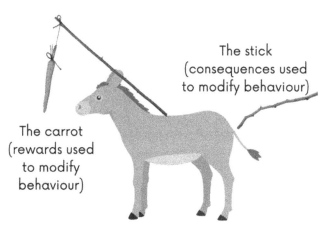

The Carrot and The Stick

The stick
(consequences used
to modify behaviour)

The carrot
(rewards used
to modify
behaviour)

Ok. On to rewards. First, children don't like reward-driven systems. No really. They don't. Ok, you don't believe me, that's fair. Why would you? Why don't you hear it from them? Scan this code and have a listen ...

Wait, what?

No really. Think about it, think about it for yourself. If or when there is a competition at school for staff how does it make *you* feel? Does it realign your core purpose of doing the best you possibly can for the children? Or, does it complicate that purpose? I know for me, when the word 'competition' is added my heart beats a little bit differently, and the thought and fear that I could possibly fail at this task overrides any other thought. Now, I am not sitting here writing this book saying I've never used rewards, oh hell no. It's actually quite the opposite. I have done every reward system you can think of: class shops, point systems, rainbow charts, stickers, prize boxes, certificates, certificate assemblies and ranking systems and anything else you might have seen on Pinterest ... trust me honey, I have tried it. Because why wouldn't I? That is all I knew when I was training. All I knew was to stick to the teachers' behaviour system, there was no module about questioning the very purpose of systems. When I started teaching it was all about blogs and Pinterest and they were absolutely cluttered with cute, colourful DIY behaviour systems that would promise to make your life as a teacher stress free. And I'm not blaming those sources either. We can only ever do what we know. We are all just doing the best we possibly can with the information that we have and that's what this book is about, new information baby.

Dig deep

In order for us to really move forward with new information we first have to honestly reflect on the use of rewards in schools and our own personal use of rewards.

Disclaimer: personal reflection can be uncomfortable. As always, I will go first. I want us to really break down what rewards we have been using and the genuine reason why we used them. We can then reflect with an unbiased lens as to how those rewards impacted our children. Often, we sweep negative thoughts of feedback in the classroom under that alphabet rug. If we don't question *what we have always done*, we can be wearing a rosy tinted lens. I want you to come and give them a scrub with me. OK, I will go first and break down three rewards I have used in the classroom.

Weather charts (a variation of a behaviour chart)

For those who don't know, the weather chart is basically a chart displaying different types of weather. Each weather represents how you are perceiving that child's behaviour in the classroom. Generally, children start in the sun. They either have their face or a name label and throughout the day the adult can direct them to move forward, backwards, up or down to different visuals depending on their behaviour. For example, a rain cloud would be a bad behaviour and a rainbow would be a good behaviour. I used this behaviour system in my six and seventh year of teaching and let me tell you why. I had been in Key Stage 2 for five years, moved to Malaysia to teach abroad and was put in Year 1. It was completely alien to me. I had never taught children at this developmental level. I was finding it tricky to manage and recommended this system. In short, I was scared. In short, it was more about control than anything else. The biggest laugh of all is that at the time I actually thought it worked. It wasn't until I really reflected that I saw the cracks. My most vulnerable children found this system so stressful that they needed a separate behaviour system. The children who were always on the rainbow, were always on rainbow. And the sunshine children? Well, now that I think about it, I did have quite a few parents email or talk to me about *how* their child could reach the rainbow. At the time I didn't think much of it, but when you put all of that together, what a shambles. Then I think about the times I really reinforced it. I can hear myself now 'Oh dear, I hope no one is going to have to move their name.' Completely innocent at the time of course but on reflection what I hear is a threat.

It didn't work because:

- the children who needed the most support became a public target;
- the children who were already behaving either weren't bothered or become highly competitive;
- I effectively created a score chart for behaviours which, if inconsistent, created more problems than solutions (especially with parents).

Raffles

So when I was in my first year of teaching I used the classic prize box and raffle system. Simple, if children showed me good behaviour, boom … they get a raffle and at the end of the week I would pick a raffle and that person gets a prize woohoo. But let's dig a little deeper, why was I using it? Or maybe a better question is when was I using it the most? That my friends is a very easy answer. Friday. I was tired, I was done with the week and was working on zero energy so suddenly I was like ok today I'm giving double raffles or Raffle Friday and it just got so ridiculous. Not to mention, expensive. When we really look at this strategy what are we doing? We are, in its purest form, conditioning children to behave the way in which we want by giving them a present or a hope of a present. What are some of the implications here? Financial, obviously, but let's consider the fact that children can work hard all week and not actually be validated. If the validation is a prize and there's only one prize it can be quite de-motivating for everyone else. Also, the goal becomes the **raffle**. Not the **learning**. And what constitutes a raffle? Is it not calling out? Is it finishing the work? Is it the same for each child? If there is a whiff of injustice children are likely to feel more resentment than motivation.

It didn't work because:

- it was expensive and inflation was unpredictable;
- it caused peer conflicts;
- children felt disappointed, jealous, angry and resentful.

Certificates and points

I was doing a point system in my class and I would reset them each week. At the beginning of the week we would have a celebration assembly where everyone got a certificate. A certificate for five points, ten points, fifteen etc. I thought it was great. Everyone wins. I genuinely wanted to celebrate all the children. But were they? Do you really want to get the five-point certificate? Do you know what happened in every single assembly? There was always one child either crying or obviously disappointed. Something I have noticed since in 'Star of the Week' assemblies. There is always one child thinking, Why didn't I do better? What did I do wrong? And if it has a negative impact on just one child's self-esteem, is it actually worth it?

It didn't work because:

- it correlated behaviour to metrics, but the metrics were subjective – all of this links to a feeling of 'unfairness/injustice';
- it created a public display of hierarchy which led to complicated feelings.

Ok, I have shared. Now I really want you to have a think. You might want to just close the book for a moment and sit with this thought. When you're ready. In the box below, think about: *What behaviour system have you tried? Why did you do it? Reflecting back now, were there any implications?*

UNPICKING WHAT BEHAVIOUR ACTUALLY IS

_____

_____

_____

_____

_____

_____

_____

_____

Let's take it to the books

What actual research and evidence is there that backs up reward-driven systems in schools? Where are we taking this from? There must be a reason we are doing it year after year, right? Well, the root of using rewards comes from the theory of behaviourism. And while I am going to refrain from leading a lecture right now, I do want to give you some headline thoughts on behaviourism.

- Behaviourism was coined around the 1920s. Yes, the 1920s. Like, the time of Gatsby. A LONG TIME AGO.
- The majority of research in behaviourism is centred around conditioning the behaviour of animals such as rats and dogs.

In all honesty, that is all I think I need to say about behaviourism! Let's update our research shall we? Now, if you are anything like I was you might not even want to hear the research LOL! The first time I read Alfie Kohn *Punished by Rewards* (Kohn 2015), I was like ... nah. Bit much. I'm not lying, it probably took me about a year to be like, Ok, I am on board. I am saying this because it is ok if you just need this information to simmer for a bit. It can be a bit of a shock when we have grown up, trained and taught in a rewards-driven system. I am going to share four concepts with you that challenge the use and effectiveness of rewards. I'm drawing on research from Alfie Kohn and Daniel H. Pink about human motivation and behaviour. Ok, deep breath … let's go.

1. Control vs motivation

When we are offering children rewards, what we accidently do is bribe them. **If** you do **this, then** you get **that**. Although we have the best intentions with rewards (on the surface) we are actively diminishing children's purpose and motivation (below the surface). Reading rewards are a great example of this. If you read five books you get a sticker. Ok, we are getting children to read. But did they enjoy the reading? Which book was their favourite? Did they identify an author they really connected with? Or do they just say 'Can I have my sticker now?' And after the stickers run out, will they still read? The research tells us, not so much. If a reward is given for a task and then you take it away, we simply won't do the task any more. It has lost its purpose. And after a while, that sticker is looking a little dull. You may need to up the ante with a smelly sticker or a 3D sticker. And therefore, the motivation was never to read more, the motivation was the reward. So we end up missing the whole point altogether by introducing the reward concept.

2. No creativity allowed

When we give children a 'no thinking' task and reward speed and effectiveness, it works. For example, sitting up straight, putting your pencil in the pot or writing your name. When we give children a problem solving, creative, higher thinking task and reward speed and effectiveness, it doesn't work. It creates panic. When we say we are rewarding creativity. It doesn't work because children are thinking 'What is their version of creativity?' Rather than actually thinking creatively. When we give children this type of task, say a maths problem and give them ideas such as cubes or coins and encourage collaboration through modelling and teaching. That is when we actually support thinking. Rewards don't support thinking. They support outcomes.

3. Going the distance

Rewards do work. Short term. You can effectively modify behaviour, yep. This my friends is a fact. But the question is, do we actually go in to teaching to control behaviour? And if it is controlled, for how long? Let's say you have a 'chatty class'. You start a reward system where children get points for putting their hand up rather than calling out. It's working. Excellent. But there are still SOME children who are finding this tricky. You decide to double the points. The children are loving it. And yet, there are still a FEW children not doing it. The children who are, start to ask 'What happens if we get the most points?' Here's the thing. Those that can, probably will anyway. Read that again. When we add rewards we really just gamify the behaviour for the children that can. They want to get to the next level. But what about those children who are not? Is it because they genuinely are trying to defy you at all costs? Or, perhaps, there is a reason why. Why are they struggling? When we use reward-heavy systems, we tend to remove the why from the algorithm and just focus on the what. **This is what you need to do to get a reward.** What happens here is some children get left behind and the other children are now focusing on the reward rather than anything else. Chasing the carrot can be either an addictive game or an unattainable goal for our students. Neither of which is actually focusing on developing the child.

4. Control vs connection

The best connections are formed mutually. We cannot force children into a positive relationship and since we know relationships are fundamental to behaviour, the use of rewards really just cancel that out. Think about that child that didn't get the stamp when they thought they were going to. That child that really thought they were getting Star of the Week. That child who always gets the most points but still doesn't feel like they have pleased you. Rewards just create complicated distractions from what is important. They create opportunities for children to win and lose, and we don't want anyone to lose on our watch. We want every child to feel like that just by being themselves, they are loved and appreciated by you.

Some other issues I have had ... If you are still on the fence

Reward once, reward always

Picture this, a child lines up quickly and receives a raffle ticket on Monday. Let's call the child Skyla. Skyla is ecstatic and thinks about it that evening. On Tuesday morning, she's ready. She lines up quickly and quietly. But this time lots of other pupils do and they get raffles but not Skyla. Hmmm, she stands up as straight as she can to get her teacher's attention. Nothing. This is what she thinks about on Tuesday evening. Wednesday morning comes and Skyla is in no rush to line up today. When we reward a child for something, they expect it every time. Why wouldn't they?

Competition becomes king

If we are using a prize box for example, it can be REALLY hard for children not be competitive, resentful and disappointed if they don't receive that glittery pen they had their eye on. None of these feelings are ones we want to trigger in our classroom. I don't know about you but I would rather children be collaborating, supporting and reflecting meaningfully instead.

Consistency can be painful

We might see all of our children sit up when we dangle a carrot but really, how long can a child sit up straight for? And what happens when we remove that carrot? Do we just have to keep dangling it for the rest of our teaching career? What if they get bored of the carrot we are dangling and need something a bit more exciting? Although I can't deny that we DO see results when using rewards, it IS short term.

Rewarding not teaching

When we create a culture of rewards the focus of what we do becomes centred around the reward rather than learning. Children become controlled by the rewards rather than focused on their own development and learning. Rewards replace a deep understanding of learning.

You're not going to like this

For me, I found that I was often leaning on rewards when I felt like children wouldn't want to do something. 'Oh it is long write day, if you do your writing you get to show the head teacher.' But actually, if children didn't want to do something, putting a reward plaster on it often made it more stressful or worse. Actually getting to the root of why was what made a difference. Better differentiation, more engaging writing tasks, different ways to present writing … these are things that instilled motivation. Not a promise of a reward.

Rewards at their worst

For reward systems, it might take us a few minutes (or weeks) to really dig deep about the damage and ineffectiveness of using them. However, there are some rewards that JUST DO NOT MAKE ANY SENSE in schools. Let me just get my rant on and please tell me these BUG you too:

Attendance – If a child is ill, they're ill. Same for adults. Don't force yourself to come in. We need to start that mindset early. Also, primary students cannot come to school independently regardless so who are we really rewarding the children or the parents?

Reading – Success is heavily linked with a child's experiences within the first five years of their life. This will impact their language, range of vocabulary and attitude towards reading. There isn't a level playing field. Children should be TAUGHT to read, not put into a league table to determine the best. Children should be inspired to read. Not shamed or bribed. Who's with me?

Spelling – Rewarding marks on a spelling test is just so old school I can't even fathom the words right now to discuss my distaste for it. However, my biggest argument for this is Coleen. I taught Coleen in Year 1 and every Monday she came in crying and physically shaking. Why? The spelling test. That is it. That is the only convincing I needed to remove any type of reward for spelling.

Homework – Those children who need it the most will need your support, not a bribe. Running a homework club would be more beneficial than ranking children's efforts at home. We have no idea what happens at home, we can't control it and it's unfair to reward pupils who have the time and support at home.

Whole body listening – Ableist. Children should be moving, children should be able to advocate for themselves about what helps them listen and learn. We shouldn't be spending our time focusing on the straightest back. DISCLAIMER: I used to do this (like a ridiculous amount). I have listened and learnt and unlearnt bad practice. There is zero shame here gang.

Uniform – I'm sorry, am I the only one exhausted by how much time we talk about uniform? Primary children cannot control whether they have the correct uniform.

Rewards at their best

If–Then rewards (as a whole-class system) are shown to be the most problematic types of rewards (Pink 2018). This reward is when you promise a child something 'If' they do something. Like 'If you finish three questions then you get a sticker' or 'If you don't call out then you can go on the iPad'. This is problematic as:

- children are often too focused on the reward to actually care about the task;
- the risk of failure means some children might opt out;
- the criteria of success makes some children feel anxious when they may have enjoyed the task;
- the reliance on a reward for a task to be successful takes away the autonomy of the task.

So that's it? Rewards are cancelled? Not so fast. Let me tell you a bit about Now–That rewards. Now–That rewards focus on recognising value and are shown to be less damaging to pupil success and can improve relationships and self-esteem (Pink 2018). This is when a child is recognised after a task but the reward is not shared beforehand. It is not a bribe. It is recognition and unexpected. These are more successful whole class because:

- children are not working towards that reward;
- children don't feel stressed about a possible reward;
- the focus is entirely on the task;
- there is an opportunity to value and recognise pupils;
- it builds relationships between the teacher and child.

It might sound like: 'Wow, you all worked so collaboratively. Why don't we all go outside for some reading?' or 'I can see you worked so hard in your writing. Why don't we photocopy your writing to show your mum today?' I love Now–That rewards. To recognise your pupils and celebrate them authentically for their learning and growth. Yes, that is what it is all about. We can do this without stickers and without prizes.

My top 10 connection-building Now-That rewards

These are some activities I might do if I want to celebrate my class as a whole. Remember, these are not promised or used as bribes. These are just nice activities to do together to recognise and celebrate your class. Note, no material rewards needed!

1.   Class game
2.   Dance party
3.   Circle time games
4.   Get the parachute out
5.   Outdoor reading
6.   Choose a story
7.   Sing a long
8.   Reading café (sit with friends, music on, shoes off)
9.   Shoes off drawing time
10. Watch a show

What is life without rewards?

Hopefully … this book. The thing is, I went straight to rewards because I wasn't given anything else in my teacher toolkit. That is what I was told and that is what I saw. But actually, behaviour isn't there for us to control. And if we want positive behaviour in our classroom, there are a number of things that contribute to that! Each with its own dedicated chapter! But if you're at this point and having a minor stress about removing all of your reward systems and unsure what this might look like. Here are some ideas …

If we take rewards away, what would be tricky? Here are two thoughts I had when removing rewards from my classroom:

1.   How will I manage children?
2.   What will I do with those really tricky behaviours?

Now unfortunately, there isn't a one solution answer. Yes I know, it's annoying. There isn't a golden ticket to behaviour. But here is a way we can start reframing it in the classroom.

If we are finding it tricky to manage the class in general we may need to develop our classroom routines and management strategies.

Classroom management vs behaviour management

For me, classroom management is about teaching the class successfully with children who are ready to learn! Behaviour management, for me, can get a bit personal and controlling. Especially in the primary classroom. It can focus too much on compliance and get a bit complicated. I am not setting out to manage anyone's behaviour other than my own. The idea for me, is that effective classroom management reduces the 'behaviour issues'. We can delve deeper into these ideas in Chapter 8, 'Behaviour and classroom management', and Chapter 7, 'Behaviour and learning'. So, what is involved in management?

How do I develop positive Classroom management?

Ms Foster

Engaging activities   Body language
Class agreement   Sensory tools
Routines   Journaling ·   Differentiation
Positive recognition   Call and Responses
     Carpet spaces   Calm spaces
Movement   Talk focused learning   Class jobs
Non verbal strategies   Supporting myself
Visual timetables   Rest   Paced activities

The tough pill to swallow

If we find that children need the rewards to do the actual work, it might be that we need to focus more on developing engagement-driven learning. This my friends can be a tough pill to swallow. What do you mean? Bored? Not engaged? How dare they! I FEEL YOU. But see it this way, you have the power to steer your ship. You are the director of this play and only YOU can engage your students in the learning. That is pretty empowering right? We are going to cover all of that in Chapter 7.

<u>A tough pill to swallow</u>

Children are off task...

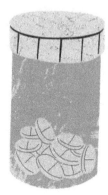

What was the task?

Behaviour management vs behaviour support

What about those children you can't seem to manage? Yes, of course, there will be times you need to manage a situation if there's a fight, or children are endangering themselves or others. But my long-term goal isn't to manage a child's behaviour. If the robust classroom systems aren't working for them, it's more likely they need to be supported and taught rather than managed. It's more likely they are lacking skills or requiring nurture. We can learn more about these children in Chapter 10, 'Behaviour and trauma', and Chapter 4, 'Behaviour and emotions'. Behaviour support is about reaching all children. If a child doesn't 'fit' into our classroom management it is not about drawing for the consequences (stay tuned for why not in the next chapter). It about drawing on our toolbox and all the amazing professionals in schools to make sure that child thrives.

What about praise?

WHAT? What is wrong with praise now? Why did I buy this book? Is that what you're thinking? Ok, praise isn't a problem. Praise isn't our enemy. But praise can be used more effectively. Like, say you got a new outfit and you ask your partner what they think and they are like 'Amazing! Love it.' Nice right? Ok, what if they said: 'Amazing, how does it feel? It looks so comfy, how did you choose it? Tell me more!' Even better, now we have some air time right?

Have you ever had a child come up into your space to show you a drawing and you say 'Oh beautiful.' But ... they don't leave and want to tell you more about it? Yep. We can use praise more effectively to empower children and develop connections. Here are some simple ideas:

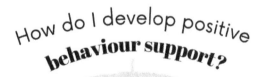

Nurture groups

conflict resolution

Working with parents

Consistency

Restorative practices

Positive Pathway

Pupil passports

Working with professionals

Now, Next   IEP

Teaching regulation

Flexible seating

Emotional literacy

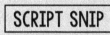

I. NOTICE

'Oooh I see you used blue for the hair. Tell me more!'
'Wow, three pages, you were really focused today!'
'Another non-fiction story! You are learning so many facts hey!'

2. ASK QUESTIONS

'I love reading this, which sentence is your favourite?'
'Wow look at this, why did you choose to draw the cat?'
'Look at this! What got you interested in planes?'

SCRIPT SNIP

3. PRAISE CHARACTER OVER OUTCOME

'Wow, you were so resilient today, I know you found that tricky, but you kept going!'
'You were super patient with that sticking and you did it!'
'I saw you listening to each other in this task, what did you learn from your teammate?'

SCRIPT SNIP

4. PUT IT BACK ON THEM

'How do you feel?'
'Do you feel proud?'
'What do you want to tell me more about?'

Even though it seems a bit scary, once you walk away from whole-class reward systems and focus more on your classroom culture and management. That is where it is AT! When we walk away from extrinsic rewards and into intrinsic motivation we are actually developing a better environment for behaviour.

TAKEAWAY BAG

- Rewards need an update.
- Research shows extrinsic rewards don't work as well as we think!
- Now–That rewards are the best type of reward.
- Instead of rewards focus on classroom management and specific behaviour support.

LIGHTS, CAMERA, ACTION REFLECTION

LIGHTS

What stood out to you in this chapter?

CAMERA

What does this look like for you right now? Tomorrow?

ACTION REFLECTION

What do you want to learn more about? What do you want to develop further?

CHAPTER 7

Behaviour and learning

Do you know what's weird? There seems to be this gaping hole of knowledge and support when it comes to behaviour and learning. Sure, you can find tonnes of training about learning pedagogies and strategies. You better believe there are lots of books out there about challenging behaviour or classroom management hacks. But ... are we talking about them both? Are we including both concepts in the same conversation? Because, they are absolutely connected. It seems kind of bizarre to me that we can spend hours of our time being disrupted by behaviour or talking about behaviour and only talking about ... behaviour. If we aren't talking about learning and behaviour we are missing the forest for the trees! In this chapter, I want to highlight some key aspects of every lesson that can either cultivate positive learning behaviours or facilitate our own behaviour nightmares!

Let's begin by reflecting on a lesson that truly stood out to you. Think of a time when you felt proud and excited to share it with your colleagues. What was it? What made the lesson so successful? Jotting down a few key points, in the box on the next page, will set the perfect tone as we delve deeper into this chapter.

Are you buying what you're selling?

I remember my teaching assistant giving me the most wonderful compliment. She said,

'You always make it fun. Like, not everyone can do that. I know
you need to teach certain things and sometimes that can be a
drag. But you do it in a way that everyone enjoys.'

In all honesty, I was in my third year of teaching and really unaware that this was a successful part of what I was doing! But a critical ingredient for me has always been fun.

UNPICKING WHAT BEHAVIOUR ACTUALLY IS

_____

_____

_____

_____

_____

_____

_____

_____

I should be having fun. I should _want_ to teach my lesson. Because if I am not enjoying it, how can I expect anyone else too? Emotional contagion. It's a thing (Nickerson 2021). It is a theory that basically shows the contagious effect of emotions. So if you are pumped and bringing that energy to your classroom. Your students not only feel it, they begin to embody it too. When we aren't feeling it? Well, we saw in the last chapter that we tend to reach for the rewards as an unconscious bribe to convince children they _want_ to do the lesson. But as we have seen, rewards only take us so far.

Tracing behaviour back to your lesson

Could the lesson be the cause of a child's behaviour? The key word being 'could' here. Unfortunately, as we have learnt, behaviour is not a clear-cut flow chart. This isn't about looking at 'absolute truths', it is about adding to the behaviour equation. As learning is often missed out from this algorithm I want to share some considerations when thinking about behaviour and learning. Let's break down how we can not only understand the root of these behaviours but also plan proactively and respond effectively to them.

The 'no' behaviour

This type of behaviour might **feel** like a child is just saying no. I am not going to do it (which can be triggering for us!). It might **look** like refusal to participate independently or collaboratively, scribbling on another child's work, having their head on the desk or refusing to move or follow the instructions.

Otto and the 'no' behaviour

I saw this behaviour with Otto EVERY SINGLE time we did a big write. Otto was super capable but he would completely shut down. Listen, as teachers I know just saying the words 'big write' conjures up a myriad of emotions. This lesson can feel like a marathon and a sprint all in one and you need to wear sweat bands just to get through it. But guess what? Some of our children dread the words too. For Otto, it took me FAR too long to realise that these behaviours manifested from low self-esteem. Otto didn't think he could do it, at least, he didn't think he could do it *well*. Sometimes when there is a 'big' project or final outcome it can seem like there is too much pressure. Children who have a fear of failure or negative experiences with *getting it wrong* may feel like opting out is the safer option. Otto would often not write a single word or lay his head on his desk in silent protest.

What's the theory here?

Let's lean into 'growth mindset' (Dweck 2017) here. This is the belief that learning is an ongoing process and intelligence is not fixed. If we support a child to develop a growth mindset they will be more willing to take risks, open to feedback and (dare I say it) excited by challenges! If you're experiencing a lot of similar behaviours in your classroom growth mindset strategies can really support this. This is very much a culture shift rather than a quick one-off strategy. It is about:

- celebrating mistakes
- teaching children about the feelings involved with resilience and perseverance
- modelling it as much as you can! (tactical mistake anyone?)
- providing specific effort-based feedback, for example:

SCRIPT SNIP

'Well done! I can see you really persevered with your spelling and spotted you looking at the sound wall!'

'I am really impressed with how you didn't give up when you forgot your words. That shows real grit!'

'What really stood out to me was how you looked around the room for different resources you could use to help you. Being resourceful is such a great skill!!!'

Where's the common sense here?

Ever felt like the least experienced in the room? Ever felt like the task was too big and would require too much energy? Ever felt like there was too much on the line? Ever felt like not doing it at all? I rest my case.

What about Otto?

So we'd get to the end of the lesson and Otto would have nothing in his book. However, he would often ask to stay and complete some during his lunch. What he was actually hoping for here was a little 1:1 pep talk from yours truly. Which of course, he received. He would then write a paragraph or two happily and head off to lunch. So? I decided to plan for this.

The proactive plan – I would aim to talk to Otto before the writing. It might be in the morning, during the carpet session or when he just got to his table. Pep talk at the ready. If possible, I would try and highlight him during the teacher-led session. The proactive positive vibes were often all Otto needed.

> ## SCRIPT SNIP
>
> *'Good Morning Otto! We have writing today and it's all about superheroes. Who is your favourite superhero?'*
> *'Otto, could you help me out? I need an adjective idea for today's lesson. How would you describe a superhero? You always have the right words!'*
> *'Oooh I just heard a great adjective from Otto, I can't wait to read your writing today.'*

But, children aren't robots and there isn't a fool proof blueprint. DAMN IT. But that's ok. We can have responsive strategies up our sleeve too. Enter: the response team. How could I support Otto if he was already stuck in the mud of self-doubt? I came across a growth mindset visual years ago and decided to develop it to interlink with emotions.

I used this with Otto and would simply ask him 'Which step are you on right now?' This was such an unthreatening question where he could point to a step or tell me. BOOM, I had a way in. A foot in the door. I would follow up with 'Let's work together to get you to the next step.' I would then offer differentiated support such as a sentence starter or a word mat. He could choose. To remove the pressure I would tell him I would circle back to him.

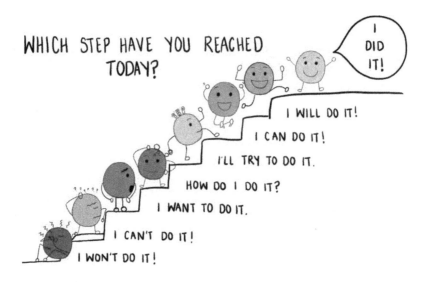

SCRIPT SNIP

'Oh my goodness, you did it. How does it feel? You've moved up a step. I didn't do it. You did. Now how shall we move up to the next step?'

And the cycle continued. As this became a habit, I would need to circle back less and less. I also noticed that this visual was highly effective for EVERYONE in the classroom to talk about their learning. So I stuck it on tables!

The 'offline' behaviour

This type of behaviour might feel like the child has detached from the lesson. They might not be completing work, talking to their partner or even looking in the right direction. Their behaviour isn't disruptive, they've just checked out a little. I often find this is most common as a plural. It's normally a chunk of the class that have gone offline rather than one or two.

Not ideal, let's face it. Remember that 'tough pill' from the last chapter? Even though we can feel personally victimised by the thought that a child doesn't enjoy our lesson, it is also kind of empowering (stay with me here). Like, ok, we know the problem. Let's create a solution. In the past, for me, this has sounded like:

- 'Oh dear, I am really disappointed with your listening.'
- 'I think we need to practise respectful listening.'
- 'Do you know the answer? No. Because you weren't listening.'

INSTEAD of going down that route, we can plan to include engagement-driven strategies. Isabella Wallace (2014) states that if children are only required to listen, their minds will wander. And if children are asked to do the same repetitive thing, their minds will wander. So instead, focus on creative opportunities for children to **do**.

Here are some ideas to get children moving in your lesson!

10 ENGAGEMENT DRIVEN STRATEGIES

GRAFFITI Q	PUZZLE IT	BALL TOSS	SCAVENGER HUNT	MEDIA MIX UP
Rather than using talk partners. Get children to answer the question or write everything they know on tables or big Flip chart paper. It get's them moving and hearing more ideas.	Rather than tell them the answers. Get them to figure it out and discover it for themselves. Have the answers or information and cut it up into puzzle pieces for children to solve in groups.	Instead of asking children. Toss a ball around. Seriously one of the easiest things to involve movement and increase engagement.	Hide the clues around the room to ignite excitement in a topic. You could also so this around the school and have a walk around! This gets children engaged and moving.	Mix it up! Talk for a bit, watch a video, read a story, have them talk, have them read...MIX up the strategies in the lesson to keep children's attention.

ENVELOPE	VISUAL STRATEGIES	GAME	OUTDOORS	WALK AND TALK
Giving children something to explore or discuss in groups? Why not give it to them in an envelope. It immediately adds intrigue!	Are you reading something out to the class? Why not get them to draw (what they see in their mind) as you are reading. This keeps their hands busy and minds buzzing. You can also do partner tasks where one partner has to explain a hidden picture for the other to draw. Great for oracy!	Can you turn it into a quiz? Can we blank out missing letters or words? Is there a relevant online game? DO IT!	Could any part of lesson be taken outdoors? This immediately activates the brain!	Swap out your partner talk for a walk and talk. Add structure by giving children signals for when to walk and when to find a partner to discuss the question.

These are some questions I ask myself when I am planning a lesson to avoid the 'offline behaviour':

1. Am I talking too much?
2. Is there a hook?
3. Is it interactive?
4. Do I find this enjoyable?

The 'wiggle wiggle' behaviour

The wiggle wiggle. Shuffling, tapping, excess fidgeting. These are my clues that I have been talking too long or I haven't provided enough movement in my lesson. Just to clarify, I allow children to move while I am teaching. I'm not talking about a little movement. I am talking about children who are obviously in NEED of more movement. This reminds me of the cinema. Remember the cinema? It was that thing before Netflix. When I go to the cinema now, I am shocked at how tricky I find it to sit still for the whole film (and not look at my phone). I know. I judge myself. But I do! That's when I start doing the wiggle wiggle. Can I twist to the side a bit? Maybe I should sit on my legs? Or stretch them way out? You might see these type of behaviours in class and more. Children might start talking or exploring that table leg that looks so shiny. Rob Plevin makes a really valid point here that leaning into what children NEED rather than your lesson plan, ultimately, saves us time in the long run (Plevin 2019). Of course, we could continue our carefully planned Bloom's Taxonomy questioning but what is likely to happen is the 'stop and start'. The 'Oh dear ...' The 'Well I'm just going to wait.' It takes a lot of courage to READ the NEEDs and take action. It might be:

Transform it
If: It feels like you're talking to a bunch of eels and learning seems impossible.
How: Change the lesson or put it on pause.

Twist it
If: The amount of wiggling is causing a negative vibe either amongst children or yourself.
How: Do a movement break! Stop and MOVE! Then get back to it.

Tweak it
If: You've noticed you've been talking for a while and have spotted a case of the wiggles.
How: Carry on but incorporate movement. Can they stand up for the next part? Can they read it in partners? Can they act it out? Can they draw it whilst you talk?

When it comes to transforming your lesson, it can be a very courageous move. But if children aren't learning, you've tried a movement break and the vibe is just OFF, it could be the right option. For example, for me, this might have been after a long (untimetabled might I add) school assembly. Let's say I had a lesson afterwards before lunch. Ergh, children will obviously be restless as well as hungry and if that lesson was heavily focused on a new concept and required more teacher-led learning ... that ain't the time. That is a moment for a transformation. Just to be clear, this level of intervention is not common otherwise we would never get around to doing anything!

The 'Goldilocks' behaviour

Goldilocks behaviour is when something is just not QUITE right. Goldilocks behaviour can show up in different ways. When thinking about making it just right we can consider three things; practicality, accessibility and academics.

As you can see, the Goldilocks behaviour isn't exactly something you can spot immediately. But, knowing this type of behaviour can support us to meet the need and apply an informed response where we might ordinarily be frustrated and react to the behaviour.

Goldilocks behaviours

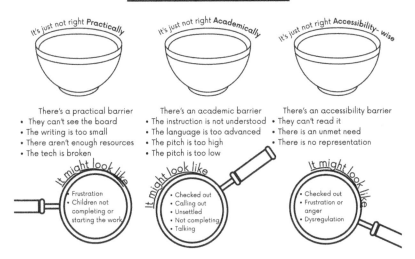

It's just not right **Practically**

There's a practical barrier
• They can't see the board
• The writing is too small
• There aren't enough resources
• The tech is broken

It's just not right **Academically**

There's an academic barrier
• The instruction is not understood
• The language is too advanced
• The pitch is too high
• The pitch is too low

It's just not right **Accessibility**- wise

There's an accessibility barrier
• They can't read it
• There is an unmet need
• There is no representation

It might look like
• Frustration
• Children not completing or starting the work

It might look like
• Checked out
• Calling out
• Unsettled
• Not completing
• Talking

It might look like
• Checked out
• Frustration or anger
• Dysregulation

Antwon and the Goldilocks behaviour

I taught Antwon in Year 6. He was working well below where he should be and I had him in a focused group to accelerate their progress. As the group came into class I had a task on the board (which they were used to). It said 'Write as many nouns as you can on your WBD.' The group seemed extra fussy and Antwon seemed to be the ringleader of this fusspot crew. He was having conversations, singing and having a giggle. I reacted. 'Antwon, what exactly are you doing? Why haven't you started?' His demeanour changed. 'I don't know what WBD is.' He seemed embarrassed.

The Goldilocks behaviour is less about being prepared for everything. And more about having a touch more curiosity. If I went in (privately) with a 'Antwon, are you ok? Do you understand the task?' I could have avoided a negative interaction and a further escalation of behaviour and disruption to the lesson. It also would have enabled me to immediately improve my practice by adding visuals to instructions.

Lewis and the Goldilocks behaviour

Do you remember Lewis from Chapter 1? It was a while back, I'll drop you the headlines, he was:

• constantly out of his seat
• constantly talking to others
• never starting his work

Because? It was WAY too easy. Lewis was working well above where he should be and was so overwhelmingly bored. Well, once I knew that I could actually plan for it rather than react to the way he was communicating it with me.

The Goldilocks behaviour can taunt us because that *perfect* differentiation is a tricky fish. I am not saying every lesson should be perfect. (Oh hell no!) What I'm saying is, the behaviour of a child may be communicating something about your lesson and it's helpful to have the Goldilocks behaviour in the back of your mind as a Google Translate kind of tool!

The 'Hunger Games' behaviour

As you know, I moved away from using extrinsic rewards in my classroom. See Chapter 6, 'Behaviour and rewards', for all the tea. This was the norm in my class. Remember that QR code I shared where children told me how they felt about the competition? Well this is what it felt like for me to watch them after saying the word 'competition' …

Welcome to the annual Hunger Games.

The class descended into chaos. Breathing became so fast paced, children started snatching and yelling at each other. I noticed a girl crying and another turning a scary shade of red.

This was all in the space of about three minutes.

After stopping the class, I found it incredibly fascinating to witness and wanted to hear their reflections about how it felt:

- 'I felt rushed.'
- 'I got really angry.'
- 'I think I forgot my manners.'
- 'I didn't care about the task.'

Well damn. You'll have seen this on Sports Day, in the playground or during PE especially. The element of competition and 'one winner' has a huge impact on behaviour. It does for adults too! Daniel H. Pink explores the idea of extrinsic motivation (Pink 2018). He highlights how recent research proves that the emphasis on use of rewards leads to unethical behaviour. Instead, Pink discusses the three drives we should be tapping into to improve intrinsic motivation. We can tap into this within the classroom.

1. Autonomy – Do children have some control over how they approach the task?
2. Mastery – Is there opportunity for children to grow and develop their skills?
3. Purpose – Is there a reason for the lesson? How is it relatable?

I know this can seem vague when planning so I wanted to share some ideas as to how we can apply the three drives in our classrooms:

Tapping into the Three Drives
...in the classroom

Purpose

Can you give a context that relates to the **school or your classroom**? Maybe it is fundraising for new playground equipment, designing decorations for the Summer Party or learning how to look after a class plant.

Can you give a context that relates to an **outcome**? Maybe they are presenting to adults or sharing with younger children. Maybe they are creating something they will then be able to use.

Can you share how the learning links to **real life or real jobs**? For example learning descriptive language can turn into a marketing challenge or even a Dragon's Den context.

Mastery

Is the learning something new? Something that builds on from what they currently know?

Is pupil feedback clear and individualised so children know how to improve?

Are there opportunities for self assessment and for pupils to set their own goals?

Are there opportunities to deepen and extend learning or are children just working towards completing a task?

Autonomy

Can children choose the outcome of what they are doing? For example, a newspaper report, story or recount?

Can children choose how they do a task? For example, collaboratively or independently?

Can children choose what they use for a task? For example, an IPAD, sentence stems or word mats?

Can children choose how they complete a task? For example, sitting in a chair, the carpet, in a 'think out loud' spot or a 'quiet' spot.

I'm not saying NEVER do a competition. But what I am saying is a competition doesn't automatically equate to better behaviour and a more successful lesson. Why do the three drives matter? Imagine a classroom where behaviour problems are nothing but a myth, where children are fully absorbed in their learning. This is the power of true engagement, where discipline and disruption fade into the background, and children thrive in their academic journey.

TAKEAWAY BAG

- There is a direct correlation between what we are teaching and behaviour.
- If you're not enjoying yourself, how can we expect our children to?
- Engagement is classroom management.
- Reading the needs in the classroom saves us time in the long run!

LIGHTS, CAMERA, ACTION REFLECTION

LIGHTS

What stood out to you in this chapter?

CAMERA

What does this look like for you right now? Tomorrow?

ACTION

What do you want to learn more about? What do you want to develop further?

Further reading

Behaviour and learning go hand in hand, and there is so much more to discover beyond this chapter. Hungry for more? Check out some of these (full details in the references):

Talk-Less Teaching by Isabella Wallace
Drive by Daniel H. Pink
The Inclusive Classroom by Daniel Sobel and Sara Alston
Attention-Grabbing Starters and Plenaries for Teachers: 99 Outrageously Engaging Activities to Increase Student Participation and Make Learning Fun (Needs-Focused Teaching Resource) by Rob Plevin

CHAPTER 8

Behaviour and classroom management

I have been looking forward to writing this chapter! The thing is, we muddle things with the term 'behaviour management' (well, I think we do). Here's why. We cannot control someone else's behaviour. We just can't and shouldn't aim to do that. It's a bit weird. But I don't think our intention is weird when we use that term. I think it is muddled because it clashes with two very big concepts; behaviour support and classroom management. These are very different things and when we treat them as the same thing, that's when things just all go a bit off key and we end up saying 'I'm fine' in that Ross from *Friends* way. If you don't know, you should Google it because it is RELATABLE. In this chapter, I am going to explain the difference and share some management strategies that support your classroom to run itself (well, almost).

What's the difference?

We touched on this in Chapter 6, 'Behaviour and rewards', but let's hone in on that language shall we? When we use the word 'management' we normally associate it with organisation, preparation, co-ordination and you know in general it is a bit of a 'tion' vibe right? Ok, so now let's think about support. What words come to mind? For me, it would be words like help, nurture or understanding. So in principle, they are just completely different approaches. Shall we play a game? I will give you some statements. I want you to tick whether you think the approach is to manage or to support. Take your time.

What is the primary approach you need?

	Support	Management
You have a big to-do list	☐	☐
Your Boss showed misconduct	☐	☐
You keep missing your bus	☐	☐
You left your planning on another laptop	☐	☐
You don't know how to plan a Phonics lesson	☐	☐
You cry after a long day	☐	☐

So for some of those, you might be thinking you need a little mixture. If you have a big to-do list, you might need support because you are feeling overwhelmed and stressed. But the actual action is management to help get you organised and realistic with what you can achieve. What you may have noticed is the support approach is more emotion driven and management is more systematic. You might also have felt that management is more proactive. Let's have a look at what this could look like in the classroom. Same game, different checklist. Take your time but do complete before skipping ahead you cheeky thing you.

What is the primary approach you need?

	Support	Management
Your classroom is messy	☐	☐
A child is not completing work	☐	☐
Everyone is talking during input	☐	☐
Equipment is being lost	☐	☐
A child is being bullied	☐	☐
A child shouts when they lose a game	☐	☐

Now here is a great distinction that I try and use. If we are talking about the class in general, it is normally a management approach. If the whole class is talking or most of the class is messy there is something I can teach and put in place to provide a solution for that. Now, I am not saying they are COMPLETELY isolated approaches but I do think it is helpful to distinguish whether the need is support or management.

The low-down

- Behaviour support focuses on individualised, emotion- and need-driven pastoral care. This can be proactive or responsive.
- Classroom management focuses on bigger group or whole-class organisation and routines that are proactively planned for and consistently reinforced.

Management and me

Management is never finished. It's never like, ok I have mastered that now … next. Because every class is different. You know you need to tweak your management if you feel like things are particularly FAFFY. The school day seems like you are constantly putting out fires and everything takes so long and you feel drained before you've started. When you achieve really effective management with a class everything just feels quite (dare I say it) effortless. Children know what they are doing, children are equal partners in running the room and you can focus more on just enjoying your job. I know, wild right?

Let me give you an example so we can really experience this FAFF together. A few years ago I taught in a Year 1 class. We had a great routine for getting the whiteboard equipment out. Children sat in rows on the carpet and at the end of the row was a tray with the whiteboards, pens and rubbers. Children would pass it down the row and sing 'Pass the whiteboards down the row' in the tune of London Bridge. Great. It worked every time and it was just a nice routine. So, when I went to another school in Year 2 I did the same routine. Why not? It was a classic. But, it just didn't stick. Children were shouting or not singing and the tray wasn't getting passed down or people wanted certain pens. I would say I tried it for about seven weeks. I was convinced if I could JUST re-teach it they would get it. But, it just didn't suit. It wasted time, I had to keep explaining again and practising again and I actually didn't want to get the whiteboards out any more. This is your reminder that if something is just feeling like a pull on your soul, it is time to switch it up. *Have you had a routine that JUST didn't work?*

UNPICKING WHAT BEHAVIOUR ACTUALLY IS

_____
_____
_____
_____
_____
_____
_____
_____

What comes under classroom management?

Anything that supports the overall running of your classroom:

How do I develop positive

Classroom management?

Ms Foster

Engaging activities

Body language

Class agreement

Sensory tools

Routines   Journaling

Differentiation

Positive recognition

Call and Responses

Carpet spaces

Calm spaces

Movement   Talk focused learning   Class jobs

Non verbal strategies

Supporting myself

Visual timetables   Rest

Paced activities

We are going to look specifically at:

- your classroom set-up
- routines
- attention getters
- reading the needs
- communication tools
- body language

When one of these pillars is missing, you feel it. Trust me. I am sharing this through many experiences of feeling the struggle. Let's explore each of these areas and top up your toolkit as we do.

Your classroom set-up

We have explored the relationship between behaviour and your classroom but what does this mean in terms of management? Really simply put, your classroom needs to be fit for purpose. When you first get your classroom there is such a sense of excitement and new home energy. Some of the technicalities and logistics can get a bit lost because you know … boring. But actually, fundamental. Here are some key thoughts:

- Can all children reach their equipment?
- Can all children push their chair in and out without hitting another?
- Can all children sit on the carpet comfortably?
- Does everyone have a coat hook or place for their belongings?
- Are labels readable and visual?
- Can children line up in the classroom safely?
- Do cupboards have a purpose and are they clearly labelled?
- Are books easily accessed?

All of these sound a bit clipboard vibes but have a big impact on management. I have taught in a class where the carpet space was SO small. Like literally I would have a child under my foot. And for me to get to the other side of the carpet, I would need a hoverboard. Why does this matter? Well, children are on the carpet almost every lesson. So that is logistically really tricky when children are squashed and crowded. And by the way, this classroom was quite big, it was just this area that was small. It wasn't a quick fix, no, it required some serious Feng Shui but it was possible. Equally, I have had a classroom where lining up meant hitting tables, knocking books etc. Every time it would cause squabbles. So? I just moved it outside the classroom. Some changes are easier to make than others but the rule still stands. If it is taking too long, find another way. As for the labels, if we want children to do more we have to help them to get there.

Routines

Have you ever had that feeling of stopping a class over and over again and wanting to scream? Have you ever felt like you can barely get through your lesson? Have you ever felt like, if you had felt like your class was completely dependent on you and your 'control'?

Yep. All of that can be resolved by REALLY good routines.

The thing is, routines aren't really given the high status they deserve. Often, there is a rush of the routines in the first week (or two if you are lucky). Children are dictated a set of rules or sweepingly told and that's it. They are expected to know. It's not made fun and rarely child friendly. **This isn't on you**, it is just the traditional legacy of routines. The norm is that sanctions are used to enforce it and 'make examples of pupils'. But actually, routines are life. If we can make a routine a daily habit ... wow. The time saved, the investment of energy. We say yes to this.

So first, what routines do you need to teach? Well I would give this a little scan.

Top routines to teach

- ☐ Lining up
- ☐ Sitting at tables
- ☐ Sitting on the carpet
- ☐ Transitions in the class
- ☐ Transitions around the school
- ☐ Talk partners
- ☐ Morning routine
- ☐ Getting equipment
- ☐ Presentation in books
- ☐ Dismissal routine
- ☐ Tidy up routine

Ms Foster

Make it an 'our' class rather than a 'your' class

One routine that has a huge impact on your classroom management is classroom jobs. I didn't want to love this strategy. Honestly, I didn't. It felt like a lot of work. But see, the alternative is YOU do everything (not fun) and it feels like your classroom. Rather than a shared classroom. If it is all on you, it is quite an impossible task. Every primary teacher can relate to terrifyingly touching something sticky in your class or angrily picking out raisins from the carpet. On an efficiency level, it is time consuming when you are the class cleaner. More than that, classroom jobs help to 'run' the day. Do you need rulers out? Do you need books collected? Are their sharp pencils available? All of this supports the flow of the day which means less dead time and more focused learning time. When children have classroom jobs there is an immediate sense of autonomy and responsibility. This sense of belonging can really be felt in the classroom and when everyone is working as a team it just MAKES SENSE.

But how?

Now, the harder question. How do you teach a routine? Here's the thing. Remember the whiteboard saga described earlier in the chapter? That's what I will call it from now on. I didn't predict my wonderful class to reject that routine! I thought it was a lifetime award routine. I was wrong. So, that is why I steer clear from telling educators HOW they should run their routines. You know your class, you know yourself, you know your classroom. I don't. You da boss. But, what I can do is share a framework I use. I call it the 4 Ps of a successful routine.

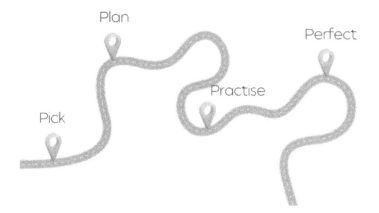

1. Pick your routine. Use the checklist above to divide and conquer!
2. Plan how you are going to do it. What do you want it to look like?
3. Practise it with your children. And allow for mistakes in this part.
4. Praise everything they are doing that is great and the impact.

When in doubt, treat routines like you would any other lesson. If you are teaching children a new sound and they mess it up, you don't get angry and say 'Oh dear. Someone wasn't listening.' You accept that this is part of the learning process and BOOM that's where we meet our friend we talked about at the beginning: support. We support them to understand and learn by, you know, teaching. Because, that is what we do babes. We teach.

Systematic management + empathy = We like.

Attention getters

I love a good attention getter. YOU NEED THEM. Don't let anyone tell you that you don't. Because they are not there on a Friday afternoon when you have decided to do an off the cuff design lesson and there is PVA EVERYWHERE and paint on the tables and it is almost home time. You NEED to be able to command the room and capture everyone's attention at the drop of a hat. You just need to. You get it.

An attention getter is quite literally an action, sound or movement that gets the attention of all pupils on the spot.

It is your job to try and experiment with different attention getters. Again, TEACH it to your children. And also, have fun with it. We should be having fun. Here are some ideas:

15 ATTENTION GETTERS

STOP SIGNAL	INSTRUMENT	RECEPTION BELL	TIMER	WIGGLE FINGERS
CLAP	RHYTHM COPY	CALL & RESPONSE	SING	VIDEO COPY
DOORBELL	TYPE IT OUT	FREEZE CONTROL	IF YOU'RE LISTENING DO XXX	QUESTION ON THE BOARD

Reading the needs

Let's think about a school. Reports are due, staff sickness is rife, assessment data is needed. A good manager and a good leader will be able to 'read the room' and see that staff need support. A good manager might say, no staff meeting today. Or, let's extend that deadline. Because a good manager knows, there is no point pulling a cart sideways. It is the same for our children, if they are in absolute awe of the snow falling outside you are probably going to let them look out the window right? Rather than close the blinds and tell them to carry on writing their story. If children have just had a long assembly and have come back to class, they probably need a movement break right? Rather than heads down back to work. It is about reading the needs of your pupils so you can be flexible and create a culture where children can thrive. Not where they are battling against the tide. I know we don't have the power to just be like 'You know what, let's learn outside ALL DAY today.' But we do actually have more power than we think. We can adjust lessons, shorten them, move them to later in the week, take them outdoors, make them collaborative, make them closed ... there is actually a lot we CAN do. So before you start a lesson or an activity just Read The Needs and ask yourself 'Are my children ready for this?' If the answer is no, why not? And what could we put in place to get them closer to yes? We can teach our little hearts out but we need our children to be present and ready to learn too.

Body language

Your body is talking before you are. So what is it saying? Is it saying the message you are wanting to say (or trying not to say)?

For example, if you are asking children to be calm, but you are breathing heavily – busying yourself and huffing and puffing – what energy is that creating?

If you are asking children to be still but you are in fact moving and doing 100 things all at once, how is that message being received?

If you are telling a student to be respectful but you are raising your voice and standing too close to them, how is that message understood?

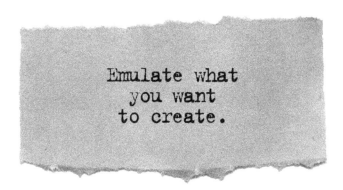

Emulate what
you want
to create.

One of the first responses to unsettled behaviour is just to move towards that child. Just to be there. Sometimes I might even hold their hand while I am teaching. But the feeling that they are seen and I am there can **sometimes** be all they need. Here are some ways you may want to make your body more of a resource in the classroom:

- Have a power position. A place you always go where you do your attention getter.
- Move towards the behaviour rather than responding with your voice.
- Circulate (if you can) during partner talk so children feel seen.
- Circulate (if you can) while teaching to keep engagement.
- Model calm breathing. (Sometimes we are doing it for real!)
- Model stillness.

Visuals

You know when you go on holiday and you don't know the language. What do you do? You look for visuals. Parking, food, the toilet etc. It puts you at ease when you have visuals.

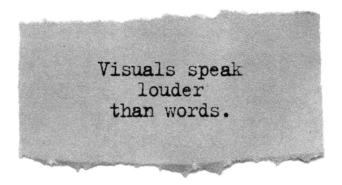

Obviously, our classroom is not like another country and if anything, we hope it becomes a home from home. But it is different. The more visuals we use, the better that communication and message is received. Even now, when I do trainings staff might say to me, 'What about older pupils?' To which I always respond, well, how would you feel if I didn't have a slideshow or any handouts today? How much more difficult would it have been? Or even enjoyable? Visuals are supportive for everyone! How might you use them in your classroom to support daily management?

- Labels
- Instructions
- Slides
- Important displays

- Books
- Table names

And what do I mean specifically by visuals? A type of picture or icon that illustrates the words.

Did I mention how much I love visual timetables?

Ok, I know we have already spoken about this. But from a classroom management point of view, I just want to hype them up again. Knowing the organisation of your day makes you feel more organised. Ok, that's all.

A moment for timers

When it comes to management, a timer has got to be part of the discussion. Timers are so great because they just are what they are. Have you ever said to a class or a child 'Two minutes' but actually it was ten minutes (or seconds)? It is confusing. It lacks consistency and our words become meaningless. Timers become this helpful third party in the classroom. I like to use timers to first set a realistic expectation. I ask children to do the routine the best that they can and we time it. That time then becomes the set expectation. Let's say it was 1 minute 23 seconds. They created it, not you. So, the next time you do that same routine you set it to 1 minute 23 seconds. Here is the beautiful thing. Not only does it set an expectation but it is also a goal they can try and beat. A class incentive that is purely about being the best they can be. 'Pure' being the key word here. No frills, no trophies, just teamwork. Now that is a concept I can get on board with.

Consistency vs let it go

This can be the confusing part where you end up having a pep talk in the mirror like 'Girl, what should we do?' It is important you are consistent with your routines. This is what I mean:

1. Once you have taught it, and they have got it. Have a word or phrase that children know that signals the routine. Even if it is just 'Tidy Up Time!' Keep it the same though.
2. Just because they know it, still spend anywhere between one to three minutes recapping your expectations. This could be showing a picture on the board or

having children remind their partners but this just supports the proactive management of it.

3. Regardless of how many times you have done it, always praise and be specific about what they are doing and the impact it is having.
4. Where possible, use visuals to help consistency. This might be a slide, a classroom display or photo.
5. Ensure ALL staff working with your class know your routines.

Now, if you are doing all of these steps and routines are STILL not working and it has been more than a few weeks it might be time to throw in the towel. Not in life, just with the routine. Have a think about why it might not be working, what you can do instead and just let it go and get back to the 4 Ps of successful routines.

TAKEAWAY BAG

- Classroom management and behaviour support are different.
- Great management means you can actually enjoy teaching.
- There isn't a tick box to perfect management but there is a roadmap!

LIGHTS, CAMERA, ACTION REFLECTION

LIGHTS

What stood out to you in this chapter?

CAMERA

What does this look like for you right now? Tomorrow?

ACTION REFLECTION

What do you want to learn more about? What do you want to develop further?

Behaviour and consequences

In this chapter we are going to unpick the intentions and reality behind using consequences in schools. It's a biggy, so buckle up!

I think before we start looking at the effectiveness of consequences in schools we just need to have a nice hard look in the mirror and think about how effective consequences are for ourselves. Think about the last consequence you remember or have experienced. Did it feel good? Did you find yourself in a place of reflection or more like irritation? It might be hard to think about the consequences we experience as adults and what that looks like. It's a bit weird isn't it? It could be staying after school because you missed the display deadline, marking your books at the weekend or it might be something a bit more obvious like being given a warning at work. As adults, we can tap into our reflective nature and you probably did find yourself thinking about what you might do next time to avoid that consequence, right? Like, yeah maybe I should have just done the display when the deadline was set. Regardless, it doesn't change the fact it's a negative vibe. Unfortunately, more often than not, negativity creates more negativity. So yes, you may have thought about your actions but you also might have snapped at your partner when you got home, sent a sassy email or said a regrettable remark. Because a consequence doesn't make you feel good. When an outcome has a negative impact on our emotions, it can make it difficult to act positively.

That can be a lot to digest so let's once again journey back to Young Jen. This time I'm in secondary school. Hey there. So consequences ... well, I had them in abundance. Here's the thing, I really didn't care what consequence I was given. You see, I struggled academically and had some emotional difficulties and experiences I was wrangling with. I didn't really want to face up to any of those, ergh, how uncomfortable. So this 'naughty' label was a welcome diversion to what was actually going on. Give them the old razzle dazzle and no one will realise I actually really needed help. That was my plan. So for me, the consequences were completely pointless. What about you? I want you to have a little think about how you felt at school about consequences. You can choose what age group you reflect on. I have no doubt it will be a different story to my own.

In the box below, consider: *What are your experiences with consequences? You might just want to write a few words or a sentence. How did they make you feel?*

UNPICKING WHAT BEHAVIOUR ACTUALLY IS

_____

_____

_____

_____

_____

_____

_____

What do we mean by consequences in school?

Do you remember when we talked about the carrot and the stick? Yep, the stick is the consequence. The stick is the threat or the punishment received for an undesired behaviour. In schools this can take many forms, such as the examples in the image on the next page.

And do you know what? I say it in every chapter. But your girl is going to say it again.

I have done this.

I've done them **all**. THIS IS NOT ABOUT SHAMING. I am not going to write a soliloquy about how guilty I am or how terrible it is. This is about sharing information as far and wide as possible and SUPPORTING educators the way I wish I was.

Let's do a little explorative activity together. Let's think about a child we have taught or who has been in school we have taught in. A child who received a lot of consequences. Picture that child in your head. Ask yourself, was the consequence what they **really** needed? Did it make a difference?

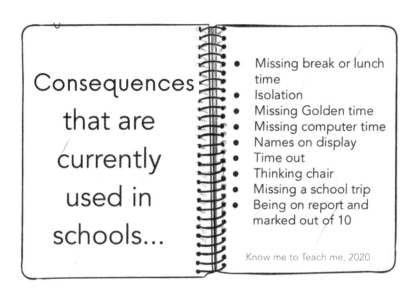

Consequences that are currently used in schools...

- Missing break or lunch time
- Isolation
- Missing Golden time
- Missing computer time
- Names on display
- Time out
- Thinking chair
- Missing a school trip
- Being on report and marked out of 10

Know me to Teach me, 2020

(Bomber, 2020)

What Vince taught me

I taught Vince in Year 6 in a specialised setting that on the cover focused on 'nurture' for our most vulnerable pupils. Vince had an extremely chaotic and traumatic home life as well as a range of different social and emotional needs. When I first started teaching Vince, his mum had told me he had just learnt to write his name (he was ten). Vince could not read and was a year away from secondary school. Vince's behaviour could range from fighting, swearing, refusal and running away. Vince was on high alert and very much experiencing a stress response much of the time. After telling you all of this, I am sure you would agree it is just nonsensical to issue consequence after consequence for surface-level behaviour. I am not saying the alternative is easy, but in all honesty, we have to agree, it doesn't really make sense does it? Vince taught me how some of the most extreme behaviours come from the most heart-wrenching places. Which leads me to my first Foster Formula:

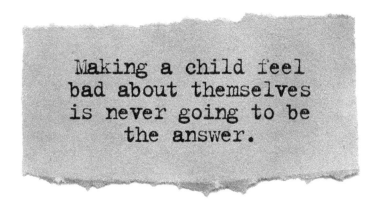

Making a child feel bad about themselves is never going to be the answer.

What Jamie taught me

I taught Jamie in Year 1 although he was a year younger than the rest of the class. Jamie's behaviour ranged from hitting to spitting or loud disruptions. Was Jamie intentionally malicious with his actions? Absolutely not. Jamie was younger. Simply put, Jamie was developmentally lacking the skill set. So again, it completely misses the point to put him on a time out. When we look at consequences alongside a context it just seems a bit odd don't you think? It is just barking up the wrong tree. Why would I punish a behaviour if a child is lacking the skill? The most obvious thing to do would be to prioritise teaching those skills. We eventually did do this, but not before I had made many mistakes trying to 'manage' this boy's development urges. All of these attempts left me exhausted and him confused!

Have a little think (box below). Can you think of a child where the consequences were just completely pointless? They didn't make any difference to the behaviour at all. You don't need to have a solution or alternative, just some consequences that OBVIOUSLY did not work.

UNPICKING WHAT BEHAVIOUR ACTUALLY IS

Something that really resonates with me is just the concept that the same children are always in detention every day. I hear this constantly from teachers and we can always name two or three children that are receiving the same consequence day after day. Obviously it isn't working for them. But this negative cycle can often lead to escalated behaviour which then leads to what? Escalated consequences. There is a term called the 'school-to-prison-pipeline' (Bomber 2020) which basically describes the process of children receiving so many disciplinary actions within education that then continues into society with no way back in. Louise Michelle Bomber says it is no surprise that there is a school-to-prison-pipeline because the root of the behaviour is never met. Our most vulnerable children experience a continual cycle of shame, punishment and judgement which will most likely continue to impact their life in a negative way. What can start out as well-intentioned zero tolerance policy can soon become a downward spiral.

Ok, but what is the actual problem?

The guard dog and consequences

Let's take it to the brain. Now let's revisit what we know about the analogy of the brain. Remember the amygdala #theguarddog? The guard dog is not a fan of consequences. Why? Because it is a type of threat and the guard dog is in charge of the threat response. That is why we suddenly feel hot and flustered if we get a sarcy email from our boss. It might be why you burst into tears during a perceived confrontation from your boss or perhaps you leave the room and slam the door. When we give children a consequence or even a threat of a consequence it can create an overwhelming emotional response.

We might think (I know I did) it is completely harmless or even needed to threaten loss of 'Golden time'. But for the child, this is not a joke. We have good intentions, we believe that by setting clear boundaries, we can correct the problematic behaviour. But what we are actually doing is drawing a battle line. Dr Daniel Siegel states that whether consequences are implicit or explicit they will almost certainly escalate emotions for the child and the adult (Payne Bryson and Siegal 2012).

Have we ditched time out yet?

We talked about time out in Chapter 4, 'Behaviour and emotions', and we are likely to talk about it again! TRUST ME, I have been there. I have put many children on time out and when I think back to it now it really was a necessity for myself. The time out was for me. I could not manage the behaviour. I didn't have any solutions. I needed to regain control. In theory, what do we hope happens on time out? Well, we hope they reflect on their behaviour and want to change their ways for good! In reality children are probably:

- plotting their revenge on you (defo me!)
- unable to compute or comprehend what happened
- feeling rubbish about themselves

In which case, it doesn't really make sense as a strategy does it? It makes children feel worse, the behaviour more complicated and nothing gets resolved. What might be better than them having a time out? Looking after yourself. If it was (like me) from a place of irritation and desperation. What can you do to support yourself? Check Chapter 14, 'Behaviour and you', for a closer look at this.

Why is removing play off the table?

Removing play is just so common isn't it? Countless times I have removed play. Whether they have been writing lines or doing a reflective form it's just a bit of a no no and here's why:

- children have a right to play, like it is their right.
- children NEED to get outside for their wellbeing.
- play time is so important for developing social skills.
- taking away play is only going to cause that child to resent the hell out of you.
- children need play time for exercise.

Not to mention that the children who normally miss their play are the ones who need to run around the most! They need to burn off that energy!

The exception files

I think it's really important to share that there are always some exceptions and we can't use blanket statements because behaviour is super complex. Here are some reasons some of my children may not have had all of their playtime at some point:

- They genuinely wanted to continue working.
- They wanted to be with a friend indoors and do an indoor activity like drawing or taking care of our class plants.
- They were too dysregulated and needed time in the calm space.
- A child had 'flipped their lid' and were unsafe at that time.
- They came in from lunch to use the calm space.
- A situation needed repairing and required a teacher or peer to peer conversation before they could go to play.

Teacher's gon' teach

Dr Becky Kennedy shares a great analogy about consequences that just puts it all into perspective for me. If a child is learning to swim and doesn't make it to their first 10m, we don't 'punish' them. We don't shout at them or put them on time out because they didn't do it (Kennedy 2022). We automatically (and rightly so) see it as developmental. We see it as learning. We talk about what they did and teach them the skills they need to develop. We don't think 'Mmm if we don't give them a consequence they won't learn and then they might grow up and not be able to swim.' We just don't. We know that making a child feel bad here will most likely worsen their progress. Because the consequence isn't the teaching part. **The teaching is.** I think this Foster Formula sums it up:

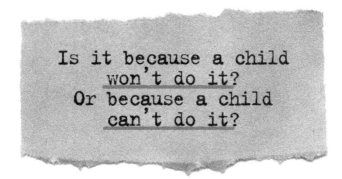

So what can we do instead?

This book? Ha! But really, if we are supporting behaviour and managing our class there is less need to draw for the consequences because things JUST RUN BETTER. But I know that is not the answer you wanted to hear right? What can you do now? What can you do tomorrow to support yourself as well as your children? I hear you. I would never stop doing something without a plan. Here are five strategies and ideas to support you to move away from the consequence ladder.

WHY?

Getting our CSI on and asking 'why?' is one of the best strategies. Rather than looking at what a child did, ask why? Why might they have done that? When we ask 'why?' we can empathise with the child and provide strategies that work! It may help to think about it in a different content. For example, if you snap at your partner, why might you do this?

- You're tired
- You feel unseen or unheard by them
- You're overwhelmed

There are lots of different reasons and of course it is dependent on the context. The same goes for our children. Bringing this Foster Formula back into our faces:

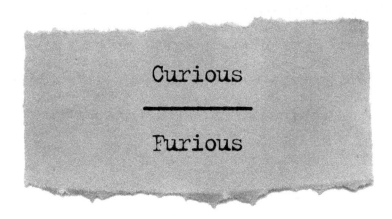

What can help us here? Check-ins! My beloved check-ins. This is a fantastic proactive tool to get to the WHY (feeling) before it becomes a WHAT (behaviour).

Teach the skills

We spend a lot of our time planning for our lessons right? I know I do. What's the learning objective? What resources will I use? Will it go in books? How will I mark it? And although these are all pretty standard and relevant, what if we added a question. How might this impact behaviour? What skills might I need to teach here? Ok fine, two questions. Let's say you are planning a partner task. How might this impact behaviour? Well they might have a peer conflict, they might be arguing over who writes, they might be unsure of who says what. What are the skills I need to teach then? Sharing, turn taking, listening etc. Remember emotional vaccines? This is a great opportunity.

So, when you are working in your pairs, how might you decide who writes first? I might say: *'Jen, would you like to write first or should I?' That would be nice wouldn't it? You may have different opinions and that is ok. I might want to use felt tips and Jen (my partner) might want to use colouring pencils. Hmmm I wonder how we could solve this? I know, what if Jen uses pencils on her part and I use felt tips on mine. That could be cool couldn't it?*

Here, we can use emotions vaccines to prepare children for different feelings by talking about them BEFORE they experience it in a safe and open space. We are giving children strategies, modelling it so they can see a real-life example and giving them the opportunity to think about possible solutions.

IT IS ALWAYS EASIER to come up with better responses when you are not IN IT. Have you ever watched a reality show and been like well obviously they are handling this all wrong! Because you are emotionally removed from it at the time. When we give children these opportunities often we build up their skillset. Other emotional vaccines we might need to model could be resilience when feeling stuck in writing or patience when working with a group.

When planning your lesson, think about the individual skills needed as well as the academic skills. That way, we can ensure those emotional vaccines are in place and children have the skillset to grow in new challenges. As Dr Becky says: Under every bad behaviour is the need for stronger emotion regulation skills.

Positive response

I remember feeling out of control with behaviour and feeling like the only solution was a consequence. Actually, there are so many things that are in our control that we can do right there and then in the classroom. I call them the 4 Rs: Remind, Recognition, Raise questions and Re-evaluate.

Let's put it into context with calling out. It can also be really tricky when you are teaching to know how to *positively* respond because, let's be honest, it is quite an emotive thing!

I don't need to say 'Jen if you call out again, that is five minutes off your play.' First, I am just going to remind them. It could just be a touch of the shoulder or a little facial expression to remind the child not to call out. You could also do a whole-class reminder, 'remember we use hands up to show respect in this class.' You could also just pause for a few seconds but don't focus your gaze on a child too much. You could carry on teaching and walk to where they are sitting and stand or sit by them as you are teaching. It is about giving children the opportunity to adjust what they are doing in a positive way.

Let's say it carries on. How annoying right? Let's think about recogniton now. This is all about re-framing through peer modelling. This is a great time to narrate and model what you WANT TO SEE, 'I love how everyone in the front row has their hand up, that is so respectful and supports us all to learn better.' I am not overdoing the praise here because it is an expectation. I am simply narrating that expectation and recognising those doing it.

SCRIPT SNIP

'I love how..' is just a great way to recognise behaviour positively.
I love how xx table are tidying up as a team.
I love how xx are taking turns.
I love how xx is patiently waiting.

NO WAY. It is carrying on? Ok, on to raise questions. If the child was still calling out after reminding and recognition, it would be time to have a little chat! STAY CURIOUS gang. There is a reason, maybe they really want you to know that they know the answer. Maybe they have low self-esteem, maybe they generally find it difficult and need support. It is our job to find out why. I would just do a partner talk or set everyone on a task so that I could speak to the child.

SCRIPT SNIP

Are you ok?
You don't seem yourself today ...
Is there anything I can do?
Do you think it would be better if ...
It's not like you to ...
Do you think you are on track?
What obstacle are you facing?
How can we bridge that together?

If you've spoken to the child and there is still calling out, stop and think. At this point, it is all about making decisions based on your questions. Could you move the child? Could you position yourself? Could you change the work they are given? Could you reposition your teaching assistant? Could you buddy them up with someone? These are all actionable steps to support that child to do the right thing. This is all about being responsive rather than reactive and thinking about what that child really needs. It might be that you speak to senior leaders after the lesson for further support.

This systematic response gives you something to follow in the classroom that focuses positively on supporting the child rather than enforcing control.

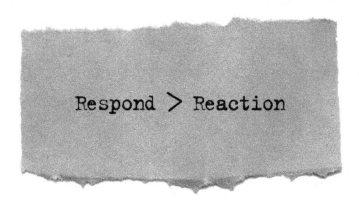

Respond > Reaction

Emotional support

We know that behaviour stems from emotions so this is where our emotional support in the classroom is fundamental. Our calm spaces and check-ins are essential strategies to proactively support children when they need it most so we are responding to their needs rather than reacting to their behaviour.

> **SCRIPT SNIP**
>
> A key point to add here is that the feelings are separate from the behaviour.
> It's ok to be angry, it is not ok to rip your book. Why don't you rip some scrap paper?
> It's ok to be angry, it is not ok to shout at me. Why don't we go to the calm space or have a walk outside?

Involving the professionals

Listen, I know what it's like. You've read up to here and you're like JEN. I have a child who hits me and I hear what you're saying but I need HELP. If a child is exhibiting extreme behaviours (behaviours that put themselves or others at risk in terms of safety) YOU MUST SEEK SUPPORT. That is very specific behaviour that requires educational professionals. Have you heard the saying 'It takes a village'? YES. I wish I had this advice because I was experiencing burnout and completely emotionally exhausted before I was told I should have informed someone. Who am I talking about?

- Your line manager
- Your SENDCo
- Educational psychologists
- School counsellors
- Your senior leadership team

There are so many educational professionals but every school is different. Please just make sure you do not deal with it alone. I was so prideful when it came to behaviour like 'Oh no I can figure it out'. Well no, I couldn't. Seeking help is a necessity. Our children need **us**, and that my friends, is a plural.

A crazy thought but ...

What if instead of consequence ladders we had intervention ladders? A consequence ladder is basically something like this:

What if instead of focusing on how we increase the punishment, we focus on how we increase the support? It might look something like this:

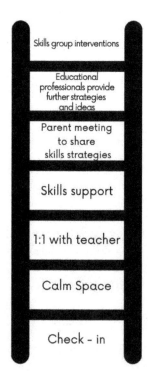

I am in no way saying this is the perfect model and every school should do this now. But what I am saying is imagine if we shifted that focus? Imagine if the goal was to equip our most vulnerable children with the skills they need rather than to scare and penalise them.

Calm scripts

I am a big fan of scripts. Because honestly, behaviour can be super triggering for us as adults. When certain behaviours elicit a strong emotional response, it can be easy to impulsively react and impose consequences without fully considering the situation. BUT scripts provide a little safety blanket here. If we know what to say, it removes the panic out of the situation. I like to use CALM scripts founded by Ginny Laleiu (a friend and colleague).

Calm stands for:

Connect (to the child);

Attune (with the emotion);

Limit (the behaviour);

Motivate and model (a solution).

I love everything about CALM scripts because they are so aligned with what we know about behaviour. We have already discussed 'Behaviour and **connection**' (Chapter 3) as well as 'Behaviour and **emotions**' (Chapter 4). A key element is 'Limits'. What won't we allow in our classroom? This isn't a free for all. One of the best things we can do for our class culture is create an agreement. An agreed set of rules or values that everyone shares.

What behaviours do we agree will support us to thrive in this classroom?

Discuss this with your children and outline together what you will *not* accept or tolerate and why. Much of this will be dependent on your school's policy too. Alongside this, we of course need to share alternatives and that is where CALM scripts are such an essential tool. They incorporate the boundary (limit) and the alternative (motivate/model) all in one package.

Let's see what this might look like in action. Stephen is quite voraciously tapping his pen.

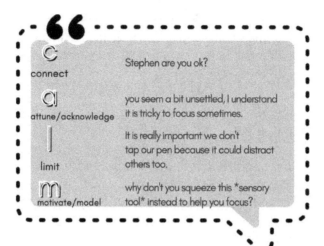

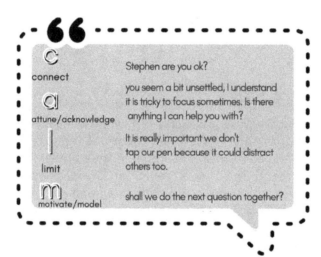

This is of course dependent on the context and what you know about Stephen!

SCRIPT SNIP

If you're looking for even less words try this:

This has happened ... What can we do now? What we are doing here is stating the behaviour and opening a dialogue.

You've scribbled on your work, what can we do now?

It might be that a child cannot offer a solution in which case we can offer ideas:

You've scribbled on your work, shall we do a new one together or would you like to do it in the calm space by yourself?

FAQs

Whenever I talk about consequences there is so much to unpick. Here are some common questions I get and responses I share.

What if a child presents dangerous behaviour?

Rather than focusing on giving consequences I would say focus on two things. How can I keep everyone safe? And what skills does this child need? This isn't necessarily the job of the teacher, it might then include other professionals. Safety is the priority. The context of each child is so different I wouldn't feel comfortable sharing individualised ideas and strategies. It is more about the mindset. Do we want to punish a child? Or are we trying to keep them safe and teach them better skills?

Are you saying to remove all consequences?

That is a pretty bold request isn't it? I am not telling schools to remove every consequence. I am just highlighting that in terms of supporting behaviour, consequences are kind of a moot point. If we are doing it we are doing it for 'policy' and 'parents' and 'structure'. It's not in the best interest of children. I know schools are more complicated than that and this isn't an overnight change. But it is something to chew on don't you think?

What if the consequence is working?

Sometimes it looks that way doesn't it? We give a consequence and a behaviour is modified. I would still suggest looking into the feelings behind the behaviour and the root. It might be that the consequence has made a child feel scared so they just do it but that is not always the whole story.

What if they should know better?

Right? I know better too. I know better than to snap at my husband or wash up before I go to bed. But sometimes, I don't. And when I don't, do I need someone to punish me? Not so much! Connection is so much stronger than correction. If I miss a meeting, there's probably a reason why and a little empathy goes a long way. Imagine if I received a warning for that? It would definitely make me spiral into negative thoughts rather than drive me to be the best I can.

Don't they need consequences because we have consequences in real life?

Yes we do have consequences in real life. But wouldn't it be more productive to teach them the skills to manage situations and reflect rather than practising getting it wrong and feeling wrong?

What about logical and natural consequences?

I think the best thing about logical and natural consequences is that they naturally make sense. If a child runs down the stairs when the rule is to walk they need to do it again properly. That is a logical consequence. If they bump into the wall, that is a natural consequence. I do think there is a place for this discussion but sometimes we can get caught up on formalising these and making sure we are doing them. For me, it misses the point. The point isn't to reprimand better, it is to build better. Channelling our air time on building better is far more productive.

We have reached the end of this chapter! How are you feeling? Do you remember that child you wrote down at the beginning of the chapter? Would you do anything differently now? Just curious!

TAKEAWAY BAG

- Consequences can trigger an overwhelming emotional response.
- Children who are supported will thrive more than children who are reprimanded.
- Teaching skills for the win!

LIGHTS, CAMERA, ACTION REFLECTION

LIGHTS

What stood out to you in this chapter?

CAMERA

What does this look like for you right now? Tomorrow?

ACTION REFLECTION

What do you want to learn more about? What do you want to develop further?

CHAPTER 10

Behaviour and trauma

Trigger Warning: *Readers who have experienced traumatic events may find the content upsetting. Please take care of yourself and consider skipping this chapter if it may cause you harm.*

'He's just a little sh*t really,' my headteacher turned and said to me. Just a few feet away Jonah, behind her, was pulling chairs to the floor. A week later I walked past a similar scene. This time with three members of the senior leadership team talking about their dinner while Jonah pushed tables around the room. 'We are just ignoring him now,' she said to me as she walked out of the room.

In this chapter we are going to unpick what trauma means, how it impacts behaviour and WHY this information is essential for every teacher entering a classroom. Trauma is a complex concept that many have dedicated their lives to writing and training about. This is a simplified snippet of what you need to know so you can support your most vulnerable pupils.

Let me tell you a bit about Jonah. Jonah wasn't in my class but he was in my school. All the teachers knew Jonah. Jonah's mother struggled with substance abuse. Jonah had witnessed domestic violence from an early age and had limited contact with his father. The contact he did have was either abusive or neglectful. Jonah had unfairly experienced traumatic experiences. Before we move forward with this chapter, can you think of a child that you have taught or has been in your school that is similar to Jonah? Maybe had a similar context or presented behaviours that no one knew how to support or manage.

In the box overleaf, note down the behaviours they presented and some information about their context.

UNPICKING WHAT BEHAVIOUR ACTUALLY IS

_____

_____

_____

_____

_____

_____

_____

_____

So what do we mean by trauma? I had the privilege of interviewing the very talented Jacolyn Norrish for this chapter. Jacolyn is the co-author for the 2021 book _Creating Trauma-Informed, Strengths-Based Classrooms: Teacher Strategies for Nurturing Students' Healing, Growth, and Learning_ (Brunzell and Norrish 2021). Jacolyn describes trauma as:

> 'An overwhelming experience that undermines a person's perception of the world as safe.'

It is an experience that rocks your very understanding of what it means to be safe. Jacci told me that she believes trauma is a mixture of what has happened to you and how your mind and body have reacted to that.

I am going to be real with you. It is hard to talk about trauma properly without knowing the different terminology and theories that surround it. I myself only truly learnt about trauma a few years ago and there is a lot of technical vocabulary that goes around it. So to save you Googling throughout this chapter I thought I would do a little vocab box you can come back to!

**Adverse childhood experience (ACE)** – Experiences that children have had that are harmful.

**Stress response** – The stress response includes **physical and thought responses to your perception of various situations**. When the stress response is turned on, your body may release substances like adrenaline and cortisol. Your organs are programmed to respond in certain ways to situations that are viewed as challenging or threatening. Just like the amygdala alarm and guard dog in Chapter 4, 'Behaviour and emotions'.

> **Toxic stress** – *Toxic stress results in prolonged activation of the stress response, with a failure of the body to recover fully.*
>
> **Window of tolerance** – *The ability in which one can tolerate before experiencing a stress response.*
>
> **Neuroception** – *Your brain's largely subconscious evaluation of the safety of a situation.*

Teachers love a checklist don't we? We like things organised and filed. Well, in the late 90s the CDC did just that. They put together a list of ten adverse childhood experiences (www.cdc.gov/violenceprevention/aces/about.html). I don't want to start up a lecture here but in summary they shared that the more ACEs (adverse childhood experiences) a child had, the more harm it caused for them later in life. This is because it impacts the wiring of their brain which means their 'guard dog' is on high alert in response to the number of threatening experiences. This, of course, impacts how they behave. Feeling in a constant state of unsafety and stress has a considerable impact on the brain and body.

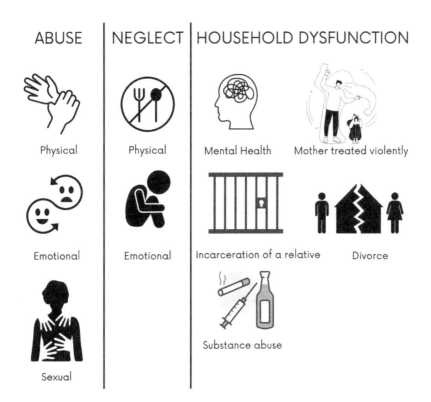

Now, as much as I love a checklist, you simply cannot put a checklist on traumatic experiences. You just can't. Yes, this is a useful guideline to help us understand the origins of traumatic experiences. However, in reality we cannot define trauma into these narrow boxes. There are so many components like child temperaments, neurodivergence and contextual information that need to be considered. Having said that, I do think the ACEs are a useful starting point to support our understanding of traumatic experiences.

So how can a traumatic experience impact a child within school? I like to use a concrete analogy to understand the impact of trauma on the brain. In all honesty, I saw this on TikTok and it really supported the way I understood it! I want to emphasise that this analogy should not be understood as a factual representation, but rather as a tool to help understand the effects.

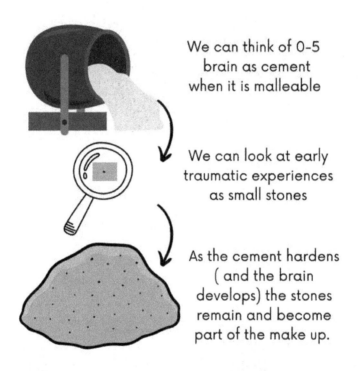

We can think of 0–5 brain as cement when it is malleable

We can look at early traumatic experiences as small stones

As the cement hardens (and the brain develops) the stones remain and become part of the make up.

This image, although visually helpful, can cause a negative mindset that there is 'no return' after trauma. This is not true. Healing is absolutely possible and this happens through a range of support that does not fall directly on your shoulders such as external therapy and counselling. Our job is not to *heal* a child. Our job is to <u>understand</u> the impact of trauma and be mindful in our approaches. What we can do is intentionally create a place of safety that is driven by student wellbeing.

When you have experienced adversity, the way your mind and body respond in life is different. Put plainly, you feel stress more deeply, more often and physiologically differently. Mona Delahooke said that behaviours can be seen as remnants of protective, defensive responses to originating events (Delahooke 2020). Basically, the behaviour is a triggered response to a traumatic experience. Feeling unsettled or unsure in the classroom could trigger responses of unsafety where the guard dog takes over in stress response. It can often take longer to de-escalate as we need to convince children that they are safe and can trust us where past experiences have wired their body to say they cannot. Ultimately, a stressed brain cannot learn. Some of the obstacles a child who has experienced ACEs might face (Brunzell and Norrish 2021):

- trouble forming relationships with teachers
- poor self-regulation
- negative thinking
- hypervigilance
- executive function challenges

So, let's take Jonah for example. It could be a different adult was in the room, the time-table changed, he didn't have breakfast that day, his uniform was dirty … it could be a number of things. He feels unsafe. His body takes over. It might be a survival response but Mona Delahook also talks about how this could be a defence response (Delahooke 2020). Protect. Protect. Protect. Jonah's past experiences have taught him to run or fight to stay safe. Jonah will not ask for help. As Child Mind Institute explains: children who have experienced trauma mask their pain with their behaviour (Miller 2022). Often, this might be big and distracting. But sometimes, it is quiet and compliant to almost be invisible. Here, I would like to draw from the incredible book *Creating Trauma-Informed, Strengths-Based Classrooms* (Brunzell and Norrish 2021) to share their insight into how trauma may present itself in the classroom. All children and circumstances are different so in no way is this a checklist activity but more of an overarching guidance to help us observe this in the classroom.

- A student who has gone through a period of instability in their relationships may develop a strong sense of independence and may seem to not require any support or help.
- A student who has been exposed to violence at home may become hypervigilant in their surroundings, constantly on the lookout for potential dangers, which can leave them with fewer cognitive resources available for learning.
- A child who has experienced neglect may engage in extreme behaviours in an attempt to gain the attention of adults and have their unmet need for care and attention fulfilled.
- A student who has been repeatedly told they are not smart or valuable may protect their self-worth by not putting any effort into their work, as a way to avoid being further judged and criticised.
- A student who lacks a sense of control or safety in their home environment may try to assert control by acting out and causing disruption at school as a way to regain a sense of control in their environment.
- A student who comes from a household where the environment is unpredictable may become highly compliant, displaying perfect behaviour in an attempt to avoid drawing attention to themselves.

For Jonah, he was most certainly a child who had no sense of control or safety at home and did whatever he could at school to feel like he had a sense of control. *What about your child that you wrote down? What do you think their behaviour was showing?*

UNPICKING WHAT BEHAVIOUR ACTUALLY IS

_____

_____

_____

_____

_____

_____

_____

_____

There is no blue-print: every child is different

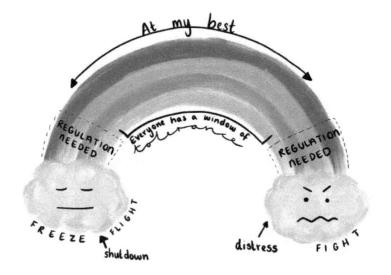

Emotional regulation means how you can effectively manage and respond to an emotion.

The image above is adapted from the 'window of tolerance' concept which was created by Dan Siegel (Payne Bryson and Siegal 2012). We touched on this in Chapter 4, 'Behaviour and emotions', but I am going to build on this by sharing a breakdown of this concept.

The rainbow

Represents the window of tolerance. This refers to how we receive and respond to emotions independently. **This window is different for everyone.** Read that again. As you can see, the rainbow has a wide span and represents a large spectrum of how we respond. But this span is different for everyone. Every child has a different window of tolerance before they need co-regulation. So it might seem like some children have a 'shorter fuse'. This is just a representation of their tolerance and needs. Jonah, for example, had a much narrower window.

Clouds

At the end of the rainbow are clouds. One cloud represents our 'Freeze or Flight' response while another represents our 'Fight' response. When an emotion cannot be tolerated we lose the ability to regulate, which means our mind and body move into survival responses. This may be different depending on the child or the context. For Jonah, it was often 'fight'.

Rainbow fringe

The end of the rainbow is where we need to support in order to regulate. In class or in parenting, this will look like co-regulation, where we support a child to re-centre. The amount we can tolerate is different for all individuals. Some children may need more support co-regulating than others.

So what can we do to support Jonah? There is a response I have heard time and time again and you might be thinking it right now too. You would be well within your right to think it, 'What about the 29 other children in the room?'

You're right. What about them? Often we give so much energy and time to some children and we feel completely drained when it is actually time to teach the others. This is not the goal. But the goal is also not to give up on our most vulnerable children. I would also say, there are more children than you think struggling in your classroom. Research conducted by the NSPCC showed that one in five children suffer from maltreatment (Radford et al. 2011). One in five. But what can you and I do about this? Right now, what can we do? The answer is new information and spreading that information as far and as wide as we can to ensure we support these children and yourself in the process.

What not to do

Trauma and consequences

We have already talked about consequences. But, what impact do consequences have on our most vulnerable pupils? If a child has experiences of trauma, their quest and need for safety feels far more urgent. This means their guard dog is much more sensitive to possible threats. So what happens here? Due to being on high alert, these children are often experiencing a stress response at school which we see in their behaviours. (See Chapter 1, 'What is behaviour?', for more). Almost unconsciously, our most vulnerable pupils become our *'most wanted'* in the education system. And how is this experience felt by our students? Well, this quote from Dr Daniel Siegel really says it all for me.

> When distressed children are isolated or excluded. The psychological need of the child goes unmet. Brain imaging shows that the experience of relational pain - like that caused by rejection - looks very similar to the experience of physical pain in terms of brain activity.

(Conkbayir 2021)

In short, punitive measures will not support these pupils. Strategies like taking away privileges and points will only reinforce a child's perspective that they are unloveable, unworthy and will push them to withdraw further. Just as we wouldn't dream of physically hurting our students as a strategy, we must completely condemn emotionally hurting our children too with traditional behaviourist approaches. Of course we do not set out to do

UNPICKING WHAT BEHAVIOUR ACTUALLY IS

_____

_____

_____

_____

_____

_____

_____

_____

this. We don't know. We aren't aware of the very real damage these approaches do. We want to help. This is what Jonah experienced. Planned ignoring, continued consequence after consequence. It was sometimes days before Jonah had actually been in the playground with his peers. He was completely dejected and had no trust in the system that was there to protect him. *Think about the child you wrote down. What strategies (no matter how well intentioned) have been used with them?*

Support yourself

I remember so clearly the first time I taught a child who had experienced things I didn't even want to say out loud. I hadn't expected to hear such stories about the students I taught. I was in my third year of teaching and was completely overwhelmed with even comprehending these experiences, let alone supporting these children. How could I support them? I was 23 years old with zero experience in trauma-informed education. It wasn't until many years later that I realised I myself had an adverse childhood experience. I didn't realise this because this language and understanding wasn't readily available to me. I had to search for it. I remember a particular occasion where I had to leave the classroom and cry in the toilet because I felt so overwhelmed with the pressure of supporting this child. I'm not the one. I can't do it. Here is what I wish I was supported with:

Come to terms with your own triggers

No, we didn't sign up for this did we? We didn't sign up to be so exposed and vulnerable, but if we don't come to terms with our own triggers we may be triggered in the classroom. I urge you to support yourself and love yourself. There is a quote that says 'Be kind, we are all healing from experiences that we don't talk about.'

Know how to breathe

I've said it before in this book and I will likely say it again! Yes, it seems simple enough but I actually didn't learn the proper breathing technique until I was pregnant. Inhale for four seconds, hold for four seconds, exhale for four seconds and repeat until calm. Try it now. See, if we are not calm our children may mirror our dysregulation. Calming yourself is crucial if we have any chance of calming our children.

Re-wire your brain

I can't do this. I can't handle this. This is our automatic response when faced with big behaviours and what we are doing here is becoming the narrator for this scene. We are deciding the tone. Change it. I can do this. I can handle this. I am brave. I am this child's consistent adult. Change the narrative.

Ask for help

Too many times I have attempted to manage behaviour that is well beyond what I should be doing. It becomes prideful. It becomes martyrdom. I will be the first to admit it. But here is a hill I will die on. Educators should not be managing behaviour where children are putting themselves or others at risk by themselves. Never. Because that happens on your watch. Because that is too much on your shoulders. And because we set ourselves up to fail, no one wins. Ask for help. Demand help. Do not do it alone.

For more support on supporting yourself check out Chapter 14, 'Behaviour and you'.

Rebuild their sense of safety in relationships

I walked past Jonah in the hallway. He was throwing a pen against a window and pulling down a display. He was absent the previous day. No one knew why. The teaching assistant outside was following what she was told and telling him how many minutes he was missing from his play to which he responded 'I don't care.' As I walked past him, my heart breaking, I put my hand on his shoulder lightly and looked him in the eye and softly said, 'I didn't see you yesterday, it is so good to see you here today.' His body softened. 'Do you want to come and chill in my classroom for a bit?' 'No,' he said quietly looking down. 'No worries, I will be in there if you want to pop in. Great to see you again Jonah.' He walked in five minutes later. I will be honest with you. I didn't have a plan. I wasn't part of his action plan at school. I wasn't part of the conversations. It wasn't a calculated strategy but an emotional call to action. I just acted instinctively. I saw a child who desperately needed love. Was that the magic bullet? Of course not. His behavioural complications didn't end with that interaction. But what if every interaction was with love and connection rather than correction? I am not saying we excuse the behaviour. But the behaviour is happening and it was only getting worse through punitive measures. A child who has experienced instability and trauma needs adults who will unconditionally stand by their side and anchor them. It is not an easy or a short solution but it is what they really need.

Focus on predictability and consistency

Predictability is security. Imagine going to a training day with no agenda. Now, imagine you had no predictability or consistency in any other area of your life. You thought this training day was going to be something you didn't have to worry about. One day where you knew what was going to happen. One day where you didn't have to be riddled with anxiety. To arrive to see there is no agenda, you don't know who is leading it, you don't know where you are sitting, how long it is, where the toilets are or who is leading what. That is a whole new feeling isn't it? A whole new horror. That is what our children may be experiencing when the visual timetable is not up. Or a supply teacher they haven't met is in the room. Perhaps it is that there is a non-uniform day they didn't know about. These can be overwhelmingly triggering for our most vulnerable children. Obviously, you and I know that schools are wild jungles! We can't possibly provide every piece of information because it does change! But what we can do is control what we can.

- Use visual timetables
- Explain the day
- Try and have consistent adults in the room
- Where this is not possible introduce the adult properly
- Tell children when you will be back if you are out of class
- Talk to children about upcoming changes in the school day as much as possible
- Where needed talk to children 1:1 about this

Provide structured choices

If a child feels like they have no sense of control in their life, structure, routine and pre-dictability is important. Structured choices can also be hugely beneficial to support children to feel like their ideas and thoughts are valued. 'Structured' being the key word here. We don't want to be like 'Hey, do you want to do English or play outside?' It is about being child-centred but not child-led. Children still need us to lead them with love as the adult.

SCRIPT SNIP

'Would you like to read your book in the book corner or by the window?'
'We have English now, would you like to use a handwriting pen or pencil today?'
'It is our maths activity now, would you like to use the worksheet or would you prefer to do it in your book?'
'It is time to line up, would you like to go at the front of the line or the back?'

Think about all those micro decisions they could make in a day and try to include them in designing their school experience where possible.

Providing communicative tools

Can you imagine experiencing overwhelmingly big feelings and not being able to say any-thing? It would feel like you are being muzzled. You would naturally want to scream, shout, run or cry. That is sometimes how our most vulnerable pupils feel. Imagine sitting on the carpet while your teacher goes through a timeline in history and you just don't know how to share that you need help. You don't know if or when you will ever receive help. For those children the only logical solution is big and extreme behaviours to gain attention and connection. But what if we could offer them something else? For me, I had two pretty simple tools that had a big impact in my classroom.

Can I talk to you?

The non-verbal signal

I had a range of non-verbal signals in my classroom. I decided to do a signal if children needed to directly talk to me about something. We discussed what the different possi-bilities this sign might mean and why it was important. I chose this gesture because children could do it quite discreetly in class by doing it at their chest. However, you may choose to do any sign you want and if I was to head back into the classroom I would prob-ably use Makaton signing (makaton.org/) (a signs and symbol programme used to aid communication) to make it as inclusive as possible. When children showed me this sign they knew I would acknowledge it and come to them at the earliest convenience, thus providing some element of consistent support.

Something you want Ms Foster to know

The box

Again, a relatively simple concept that somehow transformed my classroom. I bought a super cheap card letter box and called it the 'Something you want Ms Foster to know' box. Upon reflection this may have been a bit wordy! I explained to children it could be anything, anything they were excited about. Anything they were nervous about … anything. These broad criteria made it an appealing task. Writing to your teacher? Count me in. If it was JUST a worry box children may have felt like they needed to fabricate a worry in order to be involved in this activity and then it becomes a redundant tool doesn't it? This way, everyone can find that connection with me. Everyone is involved. It also meant children who genuinely were worried had a place to share that with me that felt safe. I had specific times where children could write and add to it and I told them I checked it at the end of every day. Therefore, not giving myself an impossible task that I couldn't fulfil. Although simple, I realised there were many children in my class silently struggling with very real things. It gave me the opportunity to intervene and support them.

For more ideas about how to support the emotions within a behaviour check out Chapter 4, 'Behaviour and emotions'.

Observational awareness

If you know you have a child who has had adverse childhood experiences, tracking their behaviours could help you identify what it looks like when they need support. Maybe it's a red prickly rash that shows up on their neck. Maybe their complexion changes or body tenses. Maybe their eyes start darting and scanning. These signs can be incredibly helpful in supporting us to intervene before a child is completely dysregulated. It might be worth printing a body map and annotating it for that child to build a contextual understanding around their needs.

In the box below, consider: *What do you think it is for the child you were thinking about?*

UNPICKING WHAT BEHAVIOUR ACTUALLY IS

_____

_____

_____

_____

_____

_____

_____

_____

Co-regulate

When Jonah is at the rainbow fringe he needs support to regulate. Often, our most vulnerable children have not had experiences where a trusted adult has modelled regulation and taught regulation. This means their regulation skills are less developed and they will need more support from us to show that and do it alongside them. This might be as simple as getting outside and going for a walk. It could be using a squeezy tool to transfer the energy or it might be curling up with noise cancelling headphones. Every child is different and there is no perfect 'How-to' for regulation. Explore different strategies and find out what works for that child. Check out Chapter 5, 'Behaviour and the classroom', to explore more about calm spaces.

TAKEAWAY BAG

- Children who have had adverse childhood experiences will behave differently in the classroom.
- This behaviour is a response to their brain wiring and how it has learnt to survive in hostile environments.
- Punitive measures will only make this behaviour worse.
- Our most vulnerable children need safety, consistency and connection.
- You should not have to manage unsafe behaviour in the classroom by yourself. Period.

I'd like to close this chapter with an African proverb:

> The Child that is
> not embraced by the
> village will burn it
> down to feel its warmth.
>
> AFRICAN PROVERB

LIGHTS, CAMERA, ACTION REFLECTION

LIGHTS

What stood out to you in this chapter?

CAMERA

What does this look like for you right now? Tomorrow?

ACTION REFLECTION

What do you want to learn more about? What do you want to develop further?

CHAPTER 11

Behaviour and bias

Don't flip past this page. This chapter is all about how we approach behaviour and how bias impacts how children thrive in education. 'Bias' is of course a big term but in this chapter I will be honing in on racial bias. I was lucky enough to interview the incredible Orlene Badu (orlenebaduconsulting.co.uk) for this chapter. Orlene is an anti-racist consultant and author of *How To Build Your Anti-Racist Classroom*.

The World Economic Forum said that when it comes to our Black British students:

> 'Teacher perceptions are seen as the biggest barrier to educational success.'

> *(World Economic Forum 2020)*

If this is brand new information to you, pour a cuppa and settle in because this chapter **needs** your attention. If this doesn't surprise you ... let's unpick this further shall we?

I want to preface this chapter by saying that this is a PROLOGUE. This is a brief summary as to how behaviour and race are intertwined in our education system to the detriment of our pupils. This is not a case study, a comprehensive guide or an in-depth journal. This really is a 'dip your toes in a dose of reality' chapter. I am not qualified or experienced enough to share anything more than that. But it was incredibly important to me that this chapter was included. I will be sharing further reading and listenings at the end of the chapter. I want to encourage you to get a little uncomfortable in this chapter. Being uncomfortable is part of the process of change and this book is all about change. Changing the way we have viewed and understood behaviour so we can do better for our children and ourselves.

Our identity

Before I present you with the cold, hard facts, let's just look inward. Let's have a think about the person reading this now. What are your experiences? How do you identify? Do you have any experience of bias in any way? When? How? What did it feel like? I, myself, am mixed race. My mumma is West Indian Jamaican, to which I am always met with gasps and 'really?' How does my experience differ to someone who is White? Well, representation was a big one for me. I remember feeling particularly ugly at primary school. The princesses were always white skinned and blue eyed and I felt that perhaps I wasn't a princess. In secondary school I became more of a commodity, more interesting. Which was odd to me. There was an ongoing sense of feeling *othered*. And now? I am mostly considered White these days, which in all honesty can be frustrating where I feel like I need to justify my race and identity. No, you don't need to know my story. No, it is not particularly noteworthy. But it is mine. It is part of my identity and impacts how I have experienced the world and how it has experienced me. It also impacts how I champion children. Who we are and who we have been **is** a part of our classroom practice whether we like it or not. We need to come to terms with this and own it. So, take a think now. It doesn't have to be anything particularly novel worthy. But, what are your experiences? How do you identify yourself?

In the box below, note down responses to these questions: *How do you identify? Have you ever experienced bias? How did that make you feel about yourself? Does it impact you as a teacher?*

UNPICKING WHAT BEHAVIOUR ACTUALLY IS

_____

_____

_____

_____

_____

_____

_____

_____

What are the facts?

Allison R. Brown stated that:

> Black bodies are policed in the streets and in the classroom.
>
> (Young 2016)

But is that true? Well, here are the facts ...

> Mixed-raced Caribbean girls are **three times more** likely to be excluded in the UK.
>
> (Mahon 2022)

> In some local authorities exclusion rates for Black Caribbean boys is **five times more** than their White peers.
>
> (McIntyre et al. 2021)

> Mixed-raced White and Black Caribbean boys are **three times more likely** to be excluded than their White peers.
>
> (Gillborn and Demack 2018)

> Research has found that Black children can be viewed as both older and less innocent than their White peers, and also falsely perceived as angry in the classroom.
>
> (Commission on Young Lives 2022)

> Further evidence from the Centre for Research in Race and Education has found that Black students are more likely to be placed in **low-ranked teaching groups**.
>
> (Commission on Young Lives 2022)

> One in five (22 per cent) of children that had ever been permanently excluded were also cautioned or sentenced for a serious violence offence.
>
> (McIntyre et al. 2021)

> **Over 40 per cent** of young people in custody are from BAME backgrounds.
>
> (Grierson 2020)

> **96 per cent** of head teachers in the UK are White men.
>
> (gov.UK 2020)

Statistics can sometimes get blurred in translation. They can seem a bit abstract and sometimes just fly past the comprehension process. I would urge you now to grab a pen and just circle or underline which statistic jumped out to you.

Hitting home

Let's zoom in on that lens. Think about your experiences at school or teaching in schools. Do the facts mirror your experiences? I remember being a teacher governor. I was 22 years old and excited about the extra responsibility. Another role? Count me in. I felt like it was a great opportunity to develop my experiences until suddenly I was on an exclusion panel. The boy was mixed race, White and Black Caribbean. He was five. He was permanently excluded. That was it. Out of the mainstream education system. I felt so confused as to how and why we couldn't support such a young and vulnerable child.

Another experience I can recall is a school who decided they would roll down the 'zero tolerance' rule. The yellow and red card system where red cards equated to temporary exclusions. In the week this was rolled out, seven exclusions were filed. As I looked at the list, every child was either Black or neurodivergent. I remember just feeling like I wanted to walk out then and there. How can we be failing children in this way? Racial bias is happening every day in schools. Do you have any experiences you recall? It might even be that you didn't think it was racial bias at the time.

In the box below, note down responses to these questions: *What experiences of racial bias have you witnessed? Did you recognise it as racial bias? How did it make you feel?*

UNPICKING WHAT BEHAVIOUR ACTUALLY IS

Terms we need to know as educators

Before we analyse the gravity of the facts, and what we can do about it, we need to level up our language around bias. We need to do this to support our Black children better. The best education is our Black voices. I would highly recommend the podcast 'Becoming an Anti-Racist Educator' where there is a supportive and safe opportunity to listen to past pupils' experiences as Black children in our educational system (www.theantiracisteducator.com/podcast).

In her TED talk, Nova Reid highlighted one of the fundamental issues we have with racial bias (Reid 2020). This is that most people are unaware of what racism is. It is mistakenly assumed to be an overt and intentional act of hate based on the colour of someone's skin. But it is much more complex than that. Here are some terms we NEED to know and understand as educators.

Microaggressions

A term used for seemingly informal verbal, behavioural or environmental slights, whether intentional or unintentional, that communicate hostile, derogatory, or negative attitudes towards culturally marginalised groups. It might be moving your bag so someone can't sit down, an eye roll or even the absence of a behaviour like not saying 'Good Morning' to someone. This is important. As Nova Reid highlighted in her Ted Talk, people who receive regular racial stress such as microaggressions can exhibit the same brain pattern as soldiers suffering from PTSD. Put plainly, it equates to trauma in the brain (Reid 2020).

Some examples of microagressions in the classroom might be:

- not pronouncing (or refusing to say) a child's name properly;
- continually excluding a child for their contributions;
- singling the same children out for behaviour (when there are several);
- demonstrating surprise at pupil success;
- a clear difference in rewards or sanctions depending on the pupil;
- choice of visuals in slides or displays (lacking diversity).

Adultification

When notions of innocence and vulnerability are not afforded to all children, certain children are treated older than their age. In the classroom, adultification might look like:

- Black children receiving harsher consequences.
- Black children receiving fewer rewards.
- Allowing (or not taking seriously) sexualised comments or behaviour towards our Black girls.
- Making assumptions on behaviour without facts.

Generational trauma

This is a term used to describe a 'passing down' of traumatic impact and emotional fall-out. In schools, we need to be mindful about the experiences of our Black parents. As horrifying as the statistics today are, imagine what they were twenty+ years ago. Probability tells us that our Black parents likely have negative connotations with schools. Of course, this is a generalisation. But we need to be aware that they may find it difficult to be in a school and/or have conversations around their child's experience in school. When communicating with our Black parents we need to ask ourselves a really simple question:

Would we communicate with our White parents in exactly the same way?

Anti-racist

Hopefully one you have heard but maybe one you have added to your school absent-mindedly. Here is a key understanding for anti-racist educators: anti-racism is a verb. It needs to be continually part of your mindset, culture and actions. What *might* anti-racism look like in schools?

- Regular coffee mornings held for BAME parents
- Regularly reviewing diversity in the curriculum
- Auditing book corners for diversity
- Regular anti-racist training for **all** staff
- Promotional opportunities for **all** staff
- Regular pupil voice surveys
- Investing in anti-racist consultancy

The facts and the reality

Let's dip back to those facts I shared and really think about the impact for our Black pupils. Exclusions essentially criminalise children. When we turn children away we tell them they cannot be helped or supported by our education system. The impact of this on their relationship and attitude to the system is shattering. Orlene warns educators to be wary of 'hidden exclusion' data and I agree with her wholeheartedly (Badu 2023). What is declared by schools is often not always the case. There are 'internal exclusions' or times where parents are asked to collect their child. There is lost data where children are being isolated from the system. This all adds to a child's experience of rejection and marginalisation. When a child comes back into the classroom, this may manifest through their behaviour. That feeling of disconnect can present itself through defiance. We've seen it in all of the Rom Coms where one person thinks the other is pulling away from the relationship so they decide to sabotage it. It is that same complex feeling and experience our children are forced to bottle up.

What do we need to be aware of when it comes to behaviour and bias?

Rosamund McNeil, assistant general secretary of the NEU teaching union, said: 'When exclusion figures show a clear disparity for Black students, it is time to ask some big questions about the curriculum, students' perspectives about what is on offer to them in school and the issues that turn young people off learning' (NEU 2020).

What do we need to consider about behaviour and bias?

The curriculum

The relationship children have with the curriculum. Can they see themselves represented? Are the themes and concepts engaging and exciting for our Black pupils? Does it offer celebrations of Black history (beyond Black history month) and high aspirations of Black students? In my mother's words:

> 'We were here, but we were painted out of history. We were made to believe we were not here and were not significant'

These are big questions and big concepts that need to be explored with your school community. This sense of belonging is crucial to children's wellbeing and relationship with school. As we know, these are key influencers of behaviour.

Identity and role models

It is human nature to be drawn to the familiar, to feel safe with familiar. Have you ever been in a situation where you are by yourself? Maybe it was a training day or a wedding but our immediate instinct is to find a friend and we normally make a quick judgement based on appearances to calculate said friend! Think about this experience for our children in schools. I remember Jai. He was a Black boy that I taught consecutively for two years. I was informing my Year 5 class that they were going to meet their Year 6 teacher for transition day. I told them his name and Jai said 'Is he White?' When I said yes he sighed and rolled his eyes. Imagine having a whole team of adults who are there to support you and none of them being the same race as you. This is important and has an impact on how safe, understood and valued our children feel. Orlene shared that children need to have role models and they need to be part of the conversation. It doesn't matter if they are the teacher, PE coach or teaching assistant. If that child has a strong connection and relationship with them they need to be involved.

Equity and assumptions

There is a really insightful research project led by Yale where teachers are asked to look at videos of children playing and proactively highlight children they felt were later going to cause behavioural issues (Brown 2016). The study showed how White teachers were looking more at the Black pupils (whom were in an Early Years setting) and 42 per cent of the teachers identified the Black boy. Although, interestingly, none of the children exhibited any behavioural concerns. What does this tell us? The feeling of being wrong before you have even started is an unimaginable experience for many. This watchful eye and ready-to-roll-out criticism undoubtedly impacts a pupil's behaviour in class. Have you ever felt like your boss doesn't like you? Or even, doesn't value you? How did it impact your performance? I can tell you right now I would feel like giving up or acting out and there really isn't much in between!

In the box below, note down your response to this question: *Which of these elements do you think your school needs to focus on to support Black pupils?*
(Multiple choice)
Curriculum   Role models   Equity and assumptions

UNPICKING WHAT BEHAVIOUR ACTUALLY IS

_____

_____

_____

_____

_____

_____

_____

_____

What can we do?

It is really important to me that there are actionable strategies but I am also so mindful that anti-racism is not a checklist. That is why these strategies are ongoing. They are more mindset shifts rather than tick boxes.

Body scan

Since bias comes from us we are the only person who has the power to stop it. Orlene advocates (Badu 2023) for all educators to actively practise doing a body scan before responding to behaviour. Acknowledging our own triggers and stressors is essential to ensuring we respond fairly. These days (fortunately) you can access body scans easily online or on Apps.

Stay proactive

All of our amazing emotional support strategies need to be applied EQUALLY. If you're doing a wellbeing check-in and a Black child has stated they need support, be proactive. Don't let it linger. If a Black child is saying they are being bullied … be proactive. Don't wait until it becomes a behaviour. Nurture the emotions. Support the wellbeing.

Stay curious

Ask yourself why? Dig deeper. If you feel like you don't have the capacity as a class teacher, ask for support from your leadership team to help you observe or to explore a behaviour incident further. It is important our Black children are not being criminalised.

Reflect often

If our Black children aren't thriving ask yourself:
Would I have responded the same way to a White pupil?
Would I have tried harder with a White pupil?

Empower Black voices

Ask questions and **listen**. Pay attention to their experiences and find ways to engage their voice. Shift from our perspective to theirs.

TAKEAWAY BAG

- Bias is real and happening every day.
- Bias has an undeniable impact on the behaviour of our Black pupils.
- Anti-racism is a verb.

LIGHTS, CAMERA, ACTION REFLECTION

LIGHTS

What stood out to you in this chapter?

CAMERA

What does this look like for you right now? Tomorrow?

ACTION REFLECTION

What do you want to learn more about? What do you want to develop further?

Further reading

Anti-racism is a verb my friends. I want to share some ready-to-go next steps for your anti-racist journey.

To read:

How to Build Your Antiracist Classroom by Orlene Badu
   Commision on Young Lives report, April 2022

To listen:

The anti-racist educator podcast

To watch:

Nova Reid 'Not all superheroes wear capes', TEDx talk

To follow:

@theblacknurserymanager
@everyday_racism

Behaviour and restorative practice

Undesirable behaviour happens. It would be foolish of me to write a book about behaviour without sharing strategies and ideas about what to do when you're in the thick of it. Restorative practice is an actionable and thoughtful strategy for approaching undesirable behaviour that focuses on growth rather than judgement. I am excited to dive into this concept with you and share what this might look like in your classroom.

You've probably gathered by now that I didn't have the BEST experiences in school. I can recall many interactions with teachers (many of whom I idolised) that left me feeling unloved. I remember a teacher calling me to the front of class and shouting at me. I remember a teacher calling me names and embarrassing me in front of a boy I had a humongous crush on (Whyyy Ms Jenks?). I remember showing a teacher something I thought was exciting (probs a stone or leaf to be fair) and she rolled her eyes and walked away. I, unfortunately, have many more of these anecdotes. Now the thing is, when I look back on these experiences, now with a teacher lens, I get it. I can see they were probably stressed, irritated or up against it. I can see that they didn't intentionally mean harm to me. But seven-year-old Jen? I felt completely alienated. I felt like I wasn't understood. Each negative interaction felt like an avalanche. And this lack of connection sent me in a different direction. I decided not to speak and later on I decided to speak in ways that got me attention. Regardless of the reception, I felt more in control. Now, I realise this can seem a bit extreme like DAMN JEN but how we choose to interact with our children is incredibly powerful. Restorative practice supports us to shape these interactions AND THE BEST PART is that mistakes are part of it. It is not about always getting it right the first time. It is about always seeking to make amends.

But, what is restorative practice?

Restorative practice is about approaching behaviour with compassion and empathy. It is centred around relationships, communication and growth. Restorative practice is about the culture we create and the discussions we have that change our understanding of behaviour.

Why do we need restorative practice?

Without restorative practice we default to consequences as a way of resolving undesirable behaviour. Now we have already explored this in Chapter 9, 'Behaviour and consequences', but let's summarise the key implications of jumping in consequence-first.

- **It fractures relationships.** Like, imagine if you missed a deadline and your boss shamed you in front of a staff meeting. How would you feel about them?
- **It doesn't teach any skills.** Let's say you always miss deadlines. What would actually help here? Perhaps a mentor or leader who shared organisation skills? Or maybe being able to observe or talk to someone who always meets deadlines early? Maybe it would be a talk with your leader about what aspects of your workload you are struggling with. The point is, if we don't find a solution it becomes a recurring negative experience for everyone involved.
- **It can be a time drainer.** Sure, at the time it feels like a quick fix. But then seventeen detentions later it can feel like the most unenjoyable real-life groundhog day.

Real life

Sometimes I am asked 'But how are you preparing children for real life? Don't we have consequences in real life?'

Here's my answer. Do we need to practise consequences? Do we need a trial run of consequences? Who does it benefit? Let's think about our real life shall we. I want you to think back to an argument you have had with your partner or a family member. Do you recall the personal consequences involved? Maybe, you ended up having a bad time at a party. Or you went to bed angry. Do we need to practise that? Bit weird isn't it?

Now, how did you and your partner or family member resolve it? Who started the conversation? How did you know you were ready to start the conversation? Did you know what to say? Was it an easy conversation or did you have to have it a few times? Was it easy to find the words? How did you respect each other's point of view? Were you able to reflect on how you behaved? Maybe even apologise? Now *that*, that is something worth practising don't you think? The restorative element to real life is how we move forward.

Five big ideas to understand restorative practice as a concept

1. We create the weather

The small interactions matter. The smile, the handshake, the comment about their party, the sincere apology, the following up when they said they had something to tell you ... the little things are big things. Sometimes new approaches can seem overwhelming. Like, don't we have enough to do? But actually, small and intentional daily habits are totally achievable. When we feel loved, safe and heard we can reflect and discuss our behaviour with the sense that we are not judged. When we don't have that security blanket and the atmosphere is a little bit frosty, we are unlikely to open up.

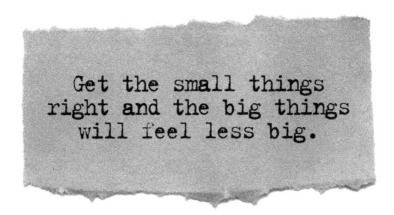

Get the small things right and the big things will feel less big.

2. We are always modelling

Children are naturally learning through watching us. The term 'mirroring' refers to how we imitate the behaviours of those closest to us. For our children, we fit into that circle. So if we want children to apologise more ... when was the last time we apologised to them? If we want children to show patience ... did we rush them coming into class or remind them politely? If we want children to take turns ... did we hog the year group iPads or did we share that our turn was finished? Think, BIG BROTHER. They are watching us. So make it count. If you rushed the teaching section and children didn't quite get the instructions and are making mistakes left, right and centre, bring them back to the carpet and acknowledge that you understand their viewpoint and recognise how you can move forward together. We are teaching ALL the time so as Ice Cube said – check yourself before you wreck yourself. Remember, the best thing about restorative practice is, it is never too late to stop, reflect and start a line of communication.

3. The impact of the 'CC'

Restorative practice is about ensuring everyone is valued and we are treating all individuals with dignity. Let me put it this way. And it has been a while since we have had a text box so make sure you grab a pen quickly.

In the box below, consider: *Have you ever had someone email you at work (about something they aren't happy with) and cc senior leadership into the email? Yes/No?*

If yes, how did it feel? Can you sum it up in a word?

If not, how would you feel about it?

EXERCISE #12.1:

_____

_____

_____

_____

_____

_____

_____

_____

Here's the thing, we all mess up. My Achilles heel is anything admin related. I am always the last person to submit data because it is just not my jam and I find it trickier to do. But I will do it. Obvs. Now, if I do mess up, how would I like to be treated? Probably the same as you. With some bloody empathy and dignity. When senior leadership are cc'd in and you are getting a digital telling-off it creates a whole Pandora's box of issues. Because now, I feel humiliated, irritated, angry and all of these emotions need to be managed and supported before I can actually do the original task. Pointless. The same thing happens for our children when we call them out. I GET IT. Time, time is of the essence. We don't mean to upset them. It might just be a 'Jen, can you stop talking.' Or 'Jen this is the third time I have reminded you.' And many more variations. The thing is, it opens that box. If we can take the time to talk about behaviour privately, it saves us time in the long run! I normally just set children on a task whether it be a partner talk, whiteboard activity or watching a video so I can address it privately. Again, this is a habit. It is about supporting yourself to facilitate that culture, not about being hard on ourselves. Being hard on ourselves or setting unachievable aspirations is never the goal!

4. Slow and steady wins the race

You know when you are feeling really heightened? Do you want to talk about it rationally right there and then? Probably not right? We have this crazy pace in schools where behaviour needs to be corrected right there on the spot, but actually if a child is experiencing some big emotions that can often make things worse. Sometimes the best solution is to pause. Give the child space while still retaining structure in your lesson. Maybe they can have some time in the calm space before both of you talk. Maybe they need to go for a walk outside with your teaching assistant. When a child is overwhelmed, it is not the right time for a teaching point. This might be between two or more children or between a child and yourself.

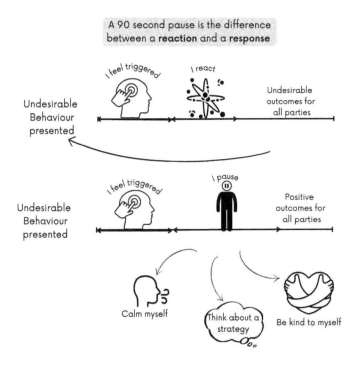

I like to convert a reaction to a response using ABC.

A – Acknowledge if I am triggered by the behaviour
B – Breathe babes
C – Connect to the pupil calmly using CALM scripts

5. With

We cannot change a child's behaviour. We just can't. Only they can do that. That is why it cannot be us vs them. It cannot be we are the boss and they just need to listen. It can't be like Matilda's dad's situation. You know the 'I'm big and you're little' vibe? It's a dead end. We need to make it collaborative. We need their perspective, their thoughts, their feelings, their input. Only together can we move forward. So, when approaching behaviour, how can we create a co-operative atmosphere?

- Listen more than we talk
- Ask open questions
- Sit in an equitable way (such as side by side, a circle, at the same height)
- Provide enough time (easier said than done I know!)
- Be solution focused rather than problem focused
- Agree rather than tell

What is a restorative conversation?

Undesirable behaviour happens. Maybe there was a fight, an argument or destruction of equipment. It happens. When it happens we can choose to issue sanctions and move on with our life or foster a restorative conversation.

Before I knew about restorative discussions I would probably approach undesirable behaviour with an 'Oh dear'. 'How disappointing'. In my first year of teaching or while training I would probably raise my voice, maybe even stand over them, I would definitely be sporting a frown. Ergh, I cringe at the thought of it. I didn't enjoy it, they didn't enjoy it. But, maybe like you, I didn't know another way. More often than not, the behaviours would happen again and I would slap on my frown and get on with the show. But ... what if there was another way?

The structure of a restorative conversation is relatively simple. Mark Finnis calls it the three bubbles (Finnis 2021):

1.   What happened?

This is the storytelling aspect. Allow the child to share their version of what happened. If there are more children, allow them to take turns and respect everyone's turn. Use prompts to support children to start processing the connections between their thoughts, feelings and behaviour.

SCRIPT SNIP
'How did you feel about that?' 'What were you thinking when that happened?'

2.   Who has been affected?

This section is normally the hardest for children. Understandably. They are thinking from their perspective. Some of the ways we can support them is to link on to parts of their story. The key here is our tone. Thinking out loud rather than accusing. Opening a discussion rather than making an assumption.

SCRIPT SNIP
'Do you think anyone else might have been upset here?' 'I wonder how xx might have felt when that happened?' 'Do you think they agreed with that?'

3.   What needs to happen now?

How do we move on? What is the future? What can we do next? This is all about coming to an agreement about a possible resolution. Our children will need our help and guidance here so be ready with some suggestions but it is key that children are equal partners. 'Hmm, how do you think we could make this better?'

I made a visual to support the structure of a restorative conversation. I would give children the visual <u>before</u> the conversation was conducted because it gave them time to really think and have some starting points.

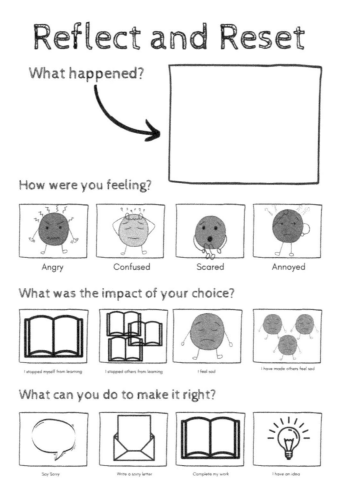

Another powerful adaptation of this was creating more open space. I printed out emotion stickers and gave children the opportunity to draw what happened (or write if they preferred), they could then browse the stickers and choose as many they felt were appropriate. This was an amazing conversation opener because I could say 'Wow, I can see you felt a lot of emotions here, can you tell me about that?' It was also a great tool for peer conflict because children could then compare their reflections while I facilitated. For example, 'I can see we were both angry.' I could also highlight similar emotions, words or drawings used.

Don't rush for a sorry

That's what we have been taught isn't it? Say sorry. Kiss and make up. It is just a traditional way to close conflict. But an insincere sorry is not well received is it? Have you ever said to a partner 'But why are you sorry?' Because you didn't feel like they truly understood your perspective? The 'understanding' is more important. It might be that the apology comes later, after the experience has been processed. Or perhaps not at all. Ergh. That is a hard pill to swallow isn't it? But remember, this is all about teaching, not punishing. The process is more important than the outcome because that is what will ultimately support the growth and change in behaviour.

The impact of a restorative conversation

What Noel taught me

Noel kept hitting children. Noel was kind, considerate and thoughtful. Noel collaborated well in class and always had a smile on his face. Noel only ever hit children in the playground. The weirdest thing was that Noel said he couldn't remember. Every time he seemed extremely distressed and would cry uncontrollably. Now, according to my boss at the time, Noel should have missed his playground for a week at least. I hated the thought of it but her argument was that children were not safe. I didn't want to put children at risk. So, I started digging. I talked to previous teachers, the SENDCo and found out Noel had a traumatic experience in his early years. When I dug a little further into the incidents, they all had one thing in common. Noel felt restricted physically. Either pushed, held down, squeezed, a hand in front of his chest ... he felt trapped which seemed to have triggered a physical response. So? By talking to him and his friends we could identify that the physical response was not ok but could source where it came from. Moving forward, they agreed to be more mindful with their body contact. Noel agreed to seek adult support or go to his playground safe space if he needed it. They understood each other. And guess what? No more hitting. Although, it seems like an overnight success story, it definitely was not that. It took months to discover the cause, identify patterns in behaviour and explicitly teach new skills to all children involved. Restorative practice isn't a plaster. But it can have a real life-changing impact.

Who's got the time?

I can almost hear myself shouting this! I HEAR YOU. Listen, I believe this is possible because I was able to do it as a full-time teacher and leader, without a teaching assistant. In order to do this, I would give children involved the visual reflection sheets. I would then curate the conversation once the rest of the class were set on a task. It takes practice but it is possible. It is made even easier if you have a teaching assistant or a school that is dedicated to investing in restorative practice. Restorative practice is a culture shift, it works best when everyone is involved but it can STILL be done by just you. I did. But remember, be your own biggest cheerleader and advocate. Small and achievable habits for the win.

Top Tips for your restorative conversation (to use with children or your partner!)

1. **Be mindful of your non-verbal communication.** How are you sitting? Standing? How is your tone communicating your message? What is your facial expression saying that your words are not? It might be that you use symbols or Makaton to ensure the conversation is equitably received.
2. **Think about the location.** Obviously, we have limited options but is it private or at least semi-private? Does it promote the ethos of value and dignity?
3. **Who can do it?** I mean, the luxury of it right? I am TOTALLY aware that actually having enough adults in the school is hard enough. I know that it is a big aspiration. But if

there is a choice of adults facilitating … try and have an adult both children know and trust. Can you imagine talking about an incident where maybe you didn't behave your best with someone you don't know? Even if you have to delay the conversation, it is probably worth thinking about.

4. **How is it conducted?** If you have a group of children, restorative practice advocates for sitting in a circle. And it makes sense doesn't it? If we think about the traditional ideology behind 'circle time' and how all voices are equal and we have rules for speaking etc.

5. **Supporting children to feel relaxed**. I like having some sensory tools available because it feels easier to talk when your hands are busy. You might also want water bottles and maybe even some biscuits if it is a tricky topic!

TAKEAWAY BAG

- Restorative practice is a culture.
- Small habits create your culture.

LIGHTS, CAMERA, ACTION REFLECTION

LIGHTS

What stood out to you in this chapter?

CAMERA

What does this look like for you right now? Tomorrow?

ACTION REFLECTION

What do you want to learn more about? What do you want to develop further?

CHAPTER 13

Behaviour and neurodiversity

In this chapter we are going to blow the lid off traditional behavioural practices and how they are most likely making behaviour **worse** in your class and are harming our neurodivergent pupils.

The word 'neurodiversity' to me, is new. It's not something I entered the profession knowing much (or anything) about. It's not something I have been trained on. And this, in itself, is why this chapter deserves to occupy space. The more I learnt about neurodiversity, the more distressed and (quite frankly) frustrated I got. How? How can this be happening? How can we be failing so many children? And why are educators still not supported, trained or equipped with the correct information and inclusive strategies? Let's give a standing ovation for behaviour and neurodiversity people because this is probably MY biggest learning curve since entering the profession and an area that continues to truly transform my practice.

I am not an expert. I am an avid learner. I feel very fortunate to have been able to interview the incredibly talented and knowledgeable Kerry Murphy for this chapter. Kerry is an author, lecturer, trainer and consultant. Kerry specialises in SEND support and I connected with Kerry a few years ago over our passion for holistic and inclusive behaviour strategies (Murphy 2022).

Let's play a game of 'Have you ever …?' I am going to make some statements and I want you to tick if they apply or resonate with you. (Full transparency: I would have ticked them all at different points of my career.)

Have you ever said …

- hands still
- eyes on me
- look at me when I am talking to you
- straight back
- stop fidgeting
- whole-body listening
- zip your lips
- no noises
- stop moving?

Have you ever thought …
  They:

- can't sit still
- can't focus
- are defiant
- won't do it
- can't listen?

If you feel like this resonates with you then hopefully by the end of this chapter you will have reframed these thoughts and this language. I hope this '**She's All That'** transformation (iconic) will stir up a behaviour renaissance and alter our thinking on behaviour approaches. To ultimately make your job easier and support **all** children to thrive.

Before we move forward, let's upskill on the terminology. As I said, many of these terms are new to me and I had to search and learn myself rather than being taught. But, these terms are important and the language we use is important. So let's get those flashcards out …

The four broad areas are named purposefully because the span of needs they cover is *broad*. For example, communication and interaction encompasses autism and speech, language and communication. In this chapter, I am not aspiring to outline the nuance of needs you may find in your classroom because the needs will be very specific and individualised to the children you work with. I don't have the authority or indeed any interest in providing specific advice. Why? First, it will never be accurate without me knowing or observing that child and may in fact be harmful. Second, I wouldn't be the person you would go to anyway. It might be your special educational needs co-ordinator, an occupational therapist, a speech and language therapist … an expert in their field. No, I don't have any intention to do that. What I want to do is share traditional strategies and approaches that happen globally in teaching and shine a light on how these can be detrimental to our neurodivergent learners. You know I love practical support and takeaways so I also plan on sharing some evergreen strategies that promote inclusivity in your classroom. At the end of this chapter, I will share some advice for further reading. Ok, now we have that out of the way. Let's start with the numbers.

What terms do we need to know?   Search

Neurotypical - Neurotypical is a term that's used to describe individuals with typical neurological development or functioning

Neurodiversity- Neurodiversity refers to diversity in the human brain and cognition, for instance in sociability, learning, attention, mood and other mental functions.

Neurdivergence - The term "neurodivergent" describes people whose brain differences affect how their brain works. That means they have different strengths and challenges from people whose brains don't have those differences.

Neuroaffirming - Is to believe that diversity and differences in how we think, feel, behave, and relate to others are what make each person unique.

Ableism - Ableism is discrimination and social prejudice against people with disabilities or who are perceived to be disabled.

4 broad areas of need -
- Cognition and Learning. ...
- Communication and Interaction. ...
- Social, Emotional and Mental Health. ...
- Sensory and/or Physical Difficulties.

Show me the numbers

Now you might be thinking, Jen is this really relevant? How is this linked to behaviour? In which case, let me hit you with some stats.

- Children with special educational needs are **five times more likely** to be suspended from school.

(The Stable Company 2020)

- Children with social, emotional and mental health needs are **fifteen times more likely** to be permanently excluded.

(NASEN 2021)

- For both of these statistics the common cause stated is **'persistent, disruptive behaviour'**.

(NASEN 2021)

What is going wrong?

If a child has additional needs, how does it make sense that they are more likely to be neglected by the system? The question in itself can be tricky to grapple with right? Well, let's think about it. How much do you know about neuro-affirming approaches? Like, in all honesty between you and me. Circle one of the below to show how confident you feel:

80–100 per cent confident

50–80 per cent confident

0–50 per cent confident

For me, I have had barely any professional development in neurodiversity in my eleven years of being a teacher and three years of training to be one. Fact. Most of what I know now (which is very much growing) is from educators who work with neurodivergent children and neurodivergent experts like Kerry Murphy. So, an undeniable barrier for me is the actual knowledge and support for educators. My experience in schools has also taught me that if a child is not diagnosed, the accommodations are little to none. And getting a child diagnosed? I mean, why don't we watch paint dry instead? Did you know that one in five children are neurodivergent? One in five (raisingchildren.net.au 2022). How many children are diagnosed in your classroom? What we tend to see in schools is neurotypical expectations and aspirations which exclude 20 per cent of our class. And when it doesn't work? It tends to be the child that is the problem. Not the approach.

The problem for me is 'one size fits all' strategies and approaches. All children have to sit *this* way, all children have to complete the work *that* way, everyone has to communicate *this* way. The cookie cutter system is unforgiving and ableist which means children are not nurtured for who they are, they are being moulded into something they are not.

What in *the Truman Show* is going on?

Ok, if you're too young for a *Truman Show* reference I'm sorry. But that is how I felt when I started to unravel the ableism approaches in our system. Why have we all been singing from the wrong hymn sheet people? So, let me share some of the approaches that are damaging to our children and why.

Whole-body listening

Whole-body listening takes a few different forms in classrooms. It's kind of like mystique you know? You might have seen Listening Larry, The 5 Ls of learning (look, lips locked, legs crossed, hands in your lap) or SLANT (Lloyd 2021) (sit up, lean forward, ask and answer questions, nod your head and track the speaker). All of which are put in place to tell children what listening must look like (and can only look like). You may have done it yourself. HELL I have. I will be the first to admit it. That's how I trained. But in reality this is nothing short of preposterous. And you know, I am not someone who just throws out 'preposterous' willy nilly but that is what it is. If you are in a staff meeting, are you all sitting in a uniform way? NAH. That is super weird. If you are on a course … do you all sit in the same way? During lockdown (sorry to bring it up) but how did you focus best? Let's let that take up some space shall we? Really think. In the box below, consider: *When you're learning, focused and content how are you sitting/laying/positioned?*

UNPICKING WHAT BEHAVIOUR ACTUALLY IS

_____

_____

_____

_____

_____

_____

_____

_____

Now, if we did an experiment and read what everyone wrote in those boxes, what is the likelihood that it would all be exactly the same? So in the words of Tag Team 'Whoop there it is.' Now, for our neurodivergent children, this is much more of an issue. It's less of a preference discussion and more of an active discomfort. When we are asking autistic pupils, for example, to sit in a uniformed way, this demand becomes so consuming that is takes first place as the primary focus. Therefore, instead of reducing barriers to learning, we end up creating one.

What Emily taught me

I taught Emily just after lockdown. Emily was autistic and her previous teacher said 'She's fine. You won't have a problem with her.', which, I found a bit odd. When I started teaching her I realised exactly what the teacher meant. She was compliant. But I also knew that she was masking. Her mum would tell me she would be completely inconsolable at home. Dysregulated, exhausted and unable to communicate. It was very clear to me that she was using all of her energy to mask all day and then exploding at home. She was also having great difficulty learning to read. As we removed the expectation of sitting on the carpet she had fewer meltdowns at home and more cognitive capacity at school. Emily was quite content sitting on a chair and using putty to help her listen. I checked in on her throughout carpet times and she was able to contribute confidently. It was about reframing what communication and listening looked like for Emily so she could be accommodated, comfortable and ENJOY learning!

Chair-based learning

Kerry Murphy (2022) says 'The biggest resource is a practitioner or teacher who dares to think beyond traditional teaching.' And that is powerful. Why are children sitting in a chair for the majority of their independent learning? Can I tell you about one of the best writing lessons I ever had? I did two things. First, I gave children three options to complete the writing. They could write their own story, do a comic strip or create their own map of a fictional place. Second, I said children could complete this in any way they felt comfortable. I had children laying on their tummy, leaning up against a chair leg, standing up … it was honestly beautiful. They were so engaged we ended up doing it for the majority of the day … whooops. But in all seriousness it was like two weeks until summer holidays so give me a break here. It was the best writing lesson I had ever done and it was right at the end of the year. Why had I formalised it so much before? Pressure? Expectations? In all honesty, I think it was just the hamster wheel of teaching. Doing the weekly write at tables was just part of the bread and butter but WOW. How different the outcomes and motivation were. Kerry shares something that I think is pretty revolutionary: chair yoga. She says, 'If you have to sit on a chair, at least make it fair.' For some of your neurodivergent children, sitting on a chair will again be incredible difficult, uncomfortable and an unnecessary barrier to learning. So if, like me, you're concerned about moving away from chairs all together here is a great strategy. Incorporating and normalising chair breaks.

   PS When writing this book, I went to a workspace studio. I went once. I COULD NOT COPE with the confinement of it! I felt so trapped. Where am I right now? Laying on my sofa baby! Proof (I hope) that we all focus differently!

Tactile body language

This was a bit of a learning curve for me. I am such a tactile person and as a child I really wished I received that tactile warmth from my teachers. So, I tried to do that for my pupils. A shoulder touch or a light cuddle. But actually, Kerry Murphy describes this as like 'live wire' for our autistic children and the fact that it is similar to a 'no skin' feeling (Murphy 2022). Can you imagine how stressful that is? Not even the touch itself but the thought that there will probably be more and how that would impact your wellbeing throughout the day. When supporting our pupils we can be mindful of body autonomy here too. Don't stand over pupils or lean in front of them. Instead, opt for a side support approach. This is less threatening, invasive and a more inclusive option.

(Visuals created by Kerry Murphy)

Behaviour charts

I mean, you know how I feel about behaviour charts and I have spoken at length within Chapter 6, 'Behaviour and rewards'. But let's take a closer look from a neuro-affirming lens. The thing is, behaviour charts are often rewarding a compliant neurotypical perspective of behaviour. Which what? Reinforcing the concept that neurotypical behaviours are favoured which you guessed it, is ableist. It means our neurodivergent children feel shamed for not behaving, communicating and expressing themselves in exactly the same way. Have you ever been in a situation where a child receives a consequence and then it escalates throughout the day? One thing after another and we might even find ourselves saying they are having a 'bad day'. But dare I say it, are they having a bad day or are we creating one for them? Eeek. I know. That was a hard pill to swallow. But we need to look at our behaviour systems the same way we mark our books. We need to assess them, reflect on them and put an ACTION in place. What we might see as misbehaviour could in fact be dysregulation or a miscommunication. Seriously.

I once had a child who just snapped at me 'And what then?' He was shrugging his shoulders and it was a blunt delivery. My teaching assistant was taken aback by this seemingly rude behaviour. I took a moment (on this occasion!) and said ... 'What do you want to know more about lovely?' He then said 'Like, what do you want us to do when we are finished.' To which I told him and he thanked me. My teaching assistant was like 'Oh my goodness he is so rude.' We talked about how actually, the way he was communicating was a little different but there is not an intention to cause offence there. Once we knew that, great, we could adapt our responses and also share alternative phrasing for him. But if we had a super strict behaviour chart? Well, he might have moved down for something like that, and can you imagine the spiral that may have followed?

Language-centred teaching

'Use your words'

'Calm down'

'Why don't you try?'

'Stop doing that'

When we use more words to try and diffuse dysregulation, more often than not, we add more distress. Especially for our autistic children that are trying to process new data to the already loading file (too many tech analogies?), less is best. Fewer words, more presence.

What strategies can we use to begin to grow a neuro-affirming classroom?

Learn

THE most important thing we can do to create an inclusive classroom is to learn. Keep learning. Every single child is different. No, I am not saying we need to create a 30-person bespoke curriculum. But what I am saying is we need to read the needs in our classroom and be responsive to that. If our children are actively uncomfortable, that is a problem. If our children are actively distressed, that is a problem. Listen to experts, listen to the children in your classroom and remember, there is no SET uniformed outline to listen, learn or communicate. Be open, be daring. Challenge the norm.

Structure and visual timetables

We have spoken about the need for visual timetables in behaviour and your classroom. But again, let's pop on our neurodiverse lens here. We know that disrupture to structure for our autistic children is more than just unsettling. It can cause high levels of anxiety. That is why visual timetables are not a nicety, they are a necessity. Ensuring these *really are* visual, easily accessed and updated are key.

Dynamic seating

We have talked about whole-body listening and chair sitting. How might you have alternatives on the carpet? And, how long are children on the carpet for? Could they do it at tables? Could they do it standing up? Walking around? Outside? These little tweaks make a huge difference to engagement and comfortability and it only takes a smidgen of thinking outside of the box!

Movement

Movement isn't a bad word. I think there is a fear that if we get children moving we can't get them to stop and we have created a problem. But actually, movement is the solution. It doesn't have to be a mini PE lesson! Movement could be anything between one minute and however long you want! It might be that you:

• ask children to stand and repeat the instructions back to you;
• do a classroom scavenger hunt;

- walk and talk instead of a partner talk sitting down;
- stop and stretch before the next learning;
- accompany language with actions;
- retell the story through yoga;
- use a YouTube guided video (check the emotions toolbox on my website!);
- using a light ball to throw and catch answers;
- use finger gym or dough disco before writing;
- allow children to skip to their tables, bunny hop or whatever you think of on the spot!;
- let them use chalk on the playground instead of writing in books;
- go to the hall to form fractions physically rather than a worksheet;
- pretend you are on a historical voyage rather than reading about it.

In the famous words of Einstein:

'Learning is experience, everything else is just information.'

When children can move TO learn, that is a powerful thing.

Calm spaces

I have spoken about calm spaces in other chapters. But let's think about that inclusive lens. Kerry shares that the whole classroom should be a calm space and I whole heartedly agree. We also discussed how the environment can be used in different ways to support different needs. Kerry talks about these as *mood zones* which very much makes sense in primary classrooms.

A space to relax: This can be your calm space. This DOES NOT need to be a branded pop-up Pinterest space. Just a calming area. You may have more than one specific area (I know I did!).

A space to react: If we know children's emotional brain is the overriding system, how are we making space for that? I remember when my son started hitting at around two. This was development and totally age appropriate. But still, I don't want to get hit! I showed him that when he felt those big angry feelings he could hit the cushion on the sofa to get it out. And you know what? He didn't even attempt to hit me again because there was a solution. Now, I am not saying it is that easy and in all honesty I had no idea it would work #parentlife but the point is, it wasn't about stopping the emotion. It was about providing a safe space for it. Is there somewhere in your room children can move? Stretch? Scrunch paper? Somewhere that allows reactions without judgement? Because the more we stifle an emotion, the trickier it gets to support.

A space to retreat: This may still be your calm space but there is an indication that they need time without interaction. Maybe a light switch? Maybe a card they stick up? I know when I am at my lowest, I really don't want to talk right away. If you try to, I will find that really hard. That's just me but lots of children will be similar. Is there accommodation for that? Could there be?

A space to resolve: I love this suggestion from Kerry. I used to have a restoration table in my room. This would be the area for talking, restoring and repairing. It might be after an incident and a child has regulated. It may be a peer conflict resolution. But it was a place of action. I had a few handouts and visuals on there but that was it.

Now I realise classrooms aren't exactly six-bedroom manor houses but, like I said, we can get creative! Use visuals, posters, tickets, lights, drapes etc. to corner off areas or make areas more dynamic to reflect the needs of our pupils.

Co-regulation

Let's revisit this with a neurodivergent perspective. Here are some inclusive approaches to consider when co-regulating your students.

- Intonation – Children will pick up on intonation so keep your tone non-threatening.
- Personal space – Remember to keep it side by side and be mindful not to be a space invader.
- Language – Less is best. A simple 'I am here' goes a long way.
- Pace – Take it slow. Slower your movements, breath and language.
- Model – Model the breathing really clearly. Model using a sensory tool alongside a pupil.

Curiosity

Is it misbehaviour or is it dysregulation? Is it defiance or demand avoidance? Is it rudeness or honesty? Is it that they aren't doing the work or they can't do the work? Ask questions. Give chances. That's it.

Neuro-affirming resources

When we are creating resources for the classroom, are they supportive of all pupils? Listen, we are all learning. If you don't know (like myself sometimes) … ask. Ask your school leaders, ask people you know who are neurodivergent, explore the neurodivergent community on social media. There are incredible experts and resources out there. I recently discovered Autism Level UP! which has a wealth of free support and resources. I want to highlight their regulation resources especially! Now, it has been a while and I haven't mentioned check-ins. How rude of me? Wellbeing check-ins need to be considered for our neurodivergent pupils. For autistic pupils, interoception (the observation of your mental state) is different. Kerry highlights the difficulty with 'naming' emotions. It is more beneficial to explore body sensations to check-in with pupils. You can use a body check chart (hes-extraordinary.com/interoception-body-check-chart) to support this, and to be honest, this is helpful for all children! A body check chart is simply drawing an outline of the body and thinking about where you feel certain emotions. You could start with hunger because children will be able to recall a growling tummy! You can find more support with this at Autism Level UP!

SCRIPT SNIP

How does your body feel?
What is your body doing right now?
What is your body telling you to do?

Processing time

Wait. Just wait. That can be one of the most effective and easy strategies we can apply. If you ask a question, give the appropriate time to answer it. I used to be terrible at the 'follow up'. It sounded a bit like this;

Context: Maths problem solving. There are pictures of items in a shop. The problem said I paid £3.55 and children have to figure out what I bought.

'What do you think the answer could be?'

1 second later … 'Have a look at the pictures at the top.'

1 second later … 'What pictures can you see?'

1 second later … 'Are you looking in the right place?'

1 second later … 'Can you see the bag of sweets picture?'

What am I doing here? I am asking four questions instead of one. I am creating five lines of thought instead of one. I am overcomplicating and adding to the cognitive load and processing time. Instead I can try:

SCRIPT SNIP

'Let's look at the pictures (while pointing to them) and think about what the answer could be.'
    Don't speak, point show a thinking processing expression and maybe start miming/modelling adding or calculating. I may even start modelling how I would work it out on the flipchart or whiteboard.
    'Join in if you like.'
    Here, I am asking one question and then scaffolding children to achieve that same question. I am trying to limit my language and instead model the process.

Teach children about neurodiversity

I often get questions like 'What if other children ask why they are allowed a fidget?' Or, 'What if they distract others when they stim?'

Yes, these are valid questions in a traditional classroom. But, when we make our classroom truly inclusive (which is a pursuit not a goal) we teach children about this in the process. We teach about how we all learn differently. We ASK about how children prefer to learn. We highlight, model and celebrate differences.

We can use books like *A Kid's Book About Autism* by Justin P. Flood and David Flood or *The Girl Who Thought in Pictures* by Dr Temple Grandin. (More on the Emotions Shelf on my website.)

We can also use incredible projects and companies. Kerry recommends the LEANS project and NeuroClastic for brilliant resources. These are free!

Specific and meaningful feedback

We are trained to praise the neurotypical standards. Positively reinforce what we 'want to see', what listening should look like, what learning should look like. The problem is this is different for all pupils and when we praise a neurotypical version we feed into an ableist narrative. So let's try celebrating children for who they are. Their character. Their strengths. This doesn't necessarily need to be specific praise but actually just noticing and affirming.

SCRIPT SNIP

'You know how you learn best!'
'I love the way you think!'
'That is such a creative way of approaching the activity.'
'It's great to respect your personal space.'
'I love how you explore!'

Final note – it takes courage

Stepping away from the norm. Standing up for your children and going against the grain. This work takes guts. It's a lot. I understand educational systems are built around many ableist approaches. Know that I trained and taught in ways I do not advocate for now. Know that the fact you have even got to the end of this chapter and are still reading shows you are ready for this. And know that your children are so lucky to have you.

TAKEAWAY BAG

- Traditional behavioural approaches are harming.
- Small changes can have a big impact.
- Seek out expert and professional advice for individual students.

LIGHTS, CAMERA, ACTION REFLECTION

LIGHTS

What stood out to you in this chapter?

CAMERA

What does this look like for you right now? Tomorrow?

ACTION REFLECTION

What do you want to learn more about? What do you want to develop further?

Further reading

A Guide to SEND in the Early Years by Kerry Murphy
Well-being and SEND by Kerry Murphy
The Inclusive Classroom by Daniel Sobel and Sarah Alston
Early Childhood and Neuroscience by Dr Mine Conkbayir

NeuroClastic neuroclastic.com/
LEANS salvesen-research.ed.ac.uk/leans
Dr Nick Walker's Key Terms neuroqueer.com/neurodiversity-terms-and-definitions/
Start Big Stay Big: 101 easy and creative ways to add movement into learning by Alison Harris www.tinkertrayplay.co.uk/product/learn-well-education-start-big-stay-big-book/

CHAPTER 14

Behaviour and you

Yes, You. In this chapter I want to talk about how you are. I want to explore the wellbeing of educators and how this is possibly the biggest factor in your classroom management and how you support behaviour.

I had the pleasure of interviewing Emily Read Daniels for this chapter, founder of the Regulated Classroom© (regulatedclassroom.com). Emily is wildly talented and passionate about supporting both pupils and teachers in the classroom, she utilises her wealth of knowledge in counselling and trauma-informed support to provide practical insights for educators.

Honestly, burnout wasn't really a word when I started teaching. At least, it wasn't a word that was used within the profession. Losing your voice or being the last person out of the building was a weird badge of honour. It was how you showed your dedication to your children. It was normal. It was normal to come in during the holidays and actually, I felt anxious if I didn't. I normalised being fully bedridden on a Saturday and working all day Sunday. It wasn't anything to cry out about. That's just teaching. Right?

There's a certain special type of anxiety associated with teaching. It's like this pocket-sized hurricane that sits on your chest on a Sunday afternoon. I don't think we need to sugar coat it. Surgeons don't. A surgeon isn't like 'Meh, it is what it is.' Because the work we do is important, it matters and there is an undeniable responsibility that we all feel right? Pretending that teachers are not feeling this is a game that no one wins.

> Experiencing 30 different
> needs at the same time
> is exhausting.
> Give yourself grace.

I personally found it a strange experience being in charge of developing young minds when to be real with you, mine myself was developing. I went into the classroom when I was twenty and research tells us that our prefrontal cortex isn't fully developed until 25 (Silverton 2021). So you know, that is kind of a mad hatter experience.

I think one thing I notice with behaviour in particular, is it seems to be this huge personal thing. We don't approach it the same as writing for example. If children aren't writing we get support, we research, we find a way. If children 'aren't behaving' … we failed. See, the way we are taught about behaviour is so inconsistent and scarce that more often than not there is this unsaid feeling like 'You either have it or you don't.' Now, that is not a nice feeling and it is also not a healthy one. I've seen so many teachers fall for this myth that we should just be able to *figure it out.* That asking for help is the first sign of failure. When really, it is the first sign of strength, boundaries and wisdom! *TES* reported that 81 per cent of teachers raised concerns about the short- and long-term impact of the pandemic on school staff (Bowyer-Crane et al. 2022) and research shows that **over 50 per cent** of teachers are leaving the profession after the first five years (Bateman 2022). Here's the thing, teachers often face situations that provoke emotions that are difficult to manage. When this happens, undoubtedly our management efforts lack effectiveness and in many cases, often work against us. Because, ultimately your vibe attracts your tribe. You are the mood ring of your classroom and what you put out there is what you will get back.

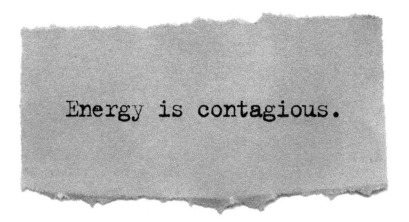

Energy is contagious.

When you are overheated or stressed you are more likely to snap, raise your voice or resort to consequences. Equally, when you are feeling low bar battery or exhausted you might be more dismissive of children and similarly impatient. What this does is trigger a negative cycle in your space as pupils respond to this energy. I like to think about it like a phone because let's face it, we are living in the digital age people and tech analogies JUST MAKE SENSE!

STRESSED   EXHAUSTED
ANGRY   LONELY
OVERWHELMED   HELPLESS

OVERHEATING   LOW BAR BATTERY

DOESN'T WORK

If we aren't enjoying what we are doing, it can feel claustrophobic and emotionally exhausting. After all, we are at school for most of our week. If it is a negative classroom climate, this can quickly feel all consuming.

I want to invite you for a little reflection. It doesn't have to be a big deep dive down memory lane with a box of tissues because, you know, let's keep it light! But I do want you to pinpoint a time when your energy was contagious. I can literally think of a time this week. My assistant head told me that they were doing parent tours and they were going to come into my classroom. My chest was immediately tighter and I felt pressured to get 'on to the work' quickly. Normally I have some sensory down time and I could feel myself rushing it. I could also feel my impatience to children not settling quick enough. That was this week, like the week I am writing this chapter, like FOR REAL. That is how often emotions creep into our classroom. So go on, just have a little think. Did you experience anything like that this week?

In the box below, note down and consider: *What did you feel? Why? How did it impact your teaching?*

UNPICKING WHAT BEHAVIOUR ACTUALLY IS

_____

_____

_____

_____

_____

_____

_____

_____

We will come back to this reflection later and apply it to our strategies so if you have been a rebel and skipped the box, go back! Ha!

Now that is just a little example but Patricia Jennings summarises the key problem here perfectly:

> If I don't notice an emotional reaction as it begins to build, it becomes difficult to regulate and I may end up doing something I regret.

> (Jennings and Siegal 2015)

I am sure we can all relate to responding to something irrationally or disproportionately either in class or life. So what can we do about it? How can we stop this negative cycle and support *ourselves* and our children better?

Toolbox time

I want to talk you through a little framework to help guide you through those moments where you are not your best self in the classroom. You are not expected to be your best self all of the time my friend. You're not a robot. But in those moments we should feel empowered and equipped to respond to our needs and get back to a regulated state. Because we simply cannot teach in a dysregulated state. It doesn't work for us, it doesn't work for our kids and it will most definitely trigger behavioural disruption. As Emily Daniels says 'Your nervous system is the biggest variable to the tone and vibe of your classroom' (regulatedclassroom.com/).

FEEL IT   SAY IT   DO IT

WITHITNESS
AND
TRACKING

I-MESSAGES
AND
MODELLING

CONNECT
ACTIVATE
SETTLE
(THE REGULATED CLASSROOM)

Feel it - how are you feeling?

Jacob Kounin found that the most effective educators were able to notice subtle changes in their students' emotions and behaviour and then proactively respond to those needs (StudyMoose 2016). He called these teachers 'with it' because they were particularly aware with what was going on in their classrooms. I say, we bring this idea of 'withitness' to ourselves. One of the WORST things we can do as an individual is to suppress our feelings or fight against them. Because, they aren't going anywhere. If we try to ignore them they will often just get bigger and take different forms. That's why my Foster Formula is...

Just feel it.

When Dr Daniel Siegel brought out his parent book he said that parents didn't really want to hear it (drdansiegel.com). Why? Because it focused on them. It wasn't a quick fix or a hack. It was about looking internally and doing that personal work. Ewww right? Well actually, that's what we are talking about here. Supporting ourselves so that we can better support our pupils. So, without further ado, let's get on with the show.

In order to acknowledge and own those feelings we first need to identify what they are. Being a teacher can sometimes feel a bit like being a hamster on a wheel. The first step to supporting ourselves is tracking how we feel. Know your triggers, know your body signals. This might feel like quite a weird concept. I remember when I first did a body scan and I was literally like YAWNFEST. I just couldn't focus and I found it tricky to just stop and pause because I had so many things on my to-do list. It's like who has the time you know? But knowing yourself doesn't have to be this arduous task. It really just starts with recognising your body sensations. So for me, if I start feeling anxious, overwhelmed or angry, it all starts in the chest. My chest suddenly feels like a brick is on top of it. I often have this fuzzy feeling too like my head feels like it is underwater. Now tune in and think back. What happens to your body? It might be that you have no clue. In which case, no stress (or pun intended). Just fold this page and come back to it when you do feel it! Take a look at mine and when you are ready, have a go at jotting your own down.

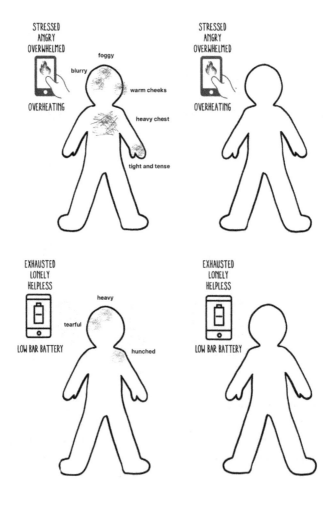

Alongside our bodily sensations you will probably notice you receive some unwelcome incoming thought traffic. It is helpful to notice these too because unwanted thoughts are quite mischievous and tend to narrate the situation at hand. Here are some thoughts you might have when you are feeling overheated or low bar battery. Circle the ones that resonate with you:

I can't do this

I give up

This is too hard

I don't want to be here

I am not able to manage this

I am a bad teacher

I am useless

I want to get out

How dare they?

I am done with this

I purposefully didn't use any full stops there because often it does feel like a constant run and flood of thoughts doesn't it? What can be helpful here is rewriting that narrative. This is almost impossible to do as improv because you are just NOT FEELING IT. Which is why a script snip can be so appreciated here. When you feel that oncoming traffic, try rewriting the scene with any of the following. Circle the ones that are giving you that positive energy:

I am capable

I am experienced

I am knowledgeable

I am kind

I am strong

I am wise

I can do this

I will do this

This is temporary

Say it – how will you communicate this?

Now we know how we are feeling, we need to own it and acknowledge this with our children. This is one of the BEST ways we can model emotional awareness and literacy. So see this as the most beautiful display of vulnerability that we can gift our children. The perfect lesson! We can use Thomas Gordon's concept of I-messaging (Adams 2012). Why?

Because it is super simple, non-judgemental and easy to remember. It is something that our children can pick up too. I-messages are simply communicating and owning our feelings. Within this we can include what we are going to do about it. I will delve a bit more into this in the 'Do it' section! Here are some examples:

Now the key thing here is we are saying it right after we feel it so we are having that immediate response to our needs. Rather than letting the feeling bubble over.

Do it – what are we going to do about it?

For this section I want to draw on the incredible framework created by Emily Read Daniels: the Regulated Classroom© (regulatedclassroom.com/pages/about-us). What I love about this framework is that it is so DAMN VALIDATING. Honestly, reading her work and talking to Emily felt so reassuring. Practices that I have been doing and demanding on prioritising in my classroom for years suddenly had a science-backed element to them. And that is my favourite place to be, somewhere in the middle of science-backed research and good old-fashioned human instinct and common sense! The Regulated Classroom© outlines four key practices educators can do to support themselves and their pupils in the classroom to experience a co-regulated state. Emily defines a practice as a *microdose* of nervous system repair intended to occur repeatedly throughout the course of the day.

Connectors – Practices that cultivate relationships. They are rooted in principles of group development and are scientifically validated benefits of play.

Activators – Rhythm-making exercises that energise the classroom. This is backed by the somatosensory perspective of regulating brainstem functioning. OH MY. That was a lot of words. It basically means it combines all of our senses to give us a strong feeling of being there in the moment.

Settlers – Practices that calm the body's stress response.

Affirmations – Encourage reflection, compassion and recognition for self and others.

We can use these practices as a response to our needs or the class needs. For example, if we are feeling low bar battery, we probably want to do some activator practices! If we are feeling overheated, we will likely need a settler. If we are feeling a sense of distance and disconnection, we might draw for a connector. These are your tools in your toolbox. These are your DO IT activities. The more we integrate them into our school day, the better for everyone because these are all about meeting human needs.

Connection

We know from Chapter 3, 'Behaviour and connection', that when we feel that sense of belonging we feel safer and happier! For more in-depth ideas on how to cultivate connection, head back to that chapter but here is a quick review of some ideas we can do with whole class:

* reading a story
* playing a game (there are SO many we can do – **check the games index!**)
* asking questions! Host a class question time
* compliment parade
* parachute games

What Zara taught me

As a leader, I was in and out of class. Zara would ask me anxiously every morning 'Are you in all day today?' She would breathe out a great sigh and her shoulders would relax if I was. Connection isn't a novelty. It's a need. A need, just like eating. We can't do two weeks of connection-building activities and then ghost our class. Our students need consistency and predictability. It impacts their feelings and behaviour if they don't get it. So don't wait to connect. Plan it in! For example, a game at the beginning of every lesson or a story after lunch or at the end of the day. Put them in your timetable so they can take up space in their own right.

Activators

The Regulated Classroom© talks about this understanding contagion where there is a power in doing something in synchrony. There is this medicinal sense of belonging when we authentically share an experience. Can you think about a time you have just been in the MOMENT with someone or a group of people? Maybe you were talking about *Game of Thrones* or maybe you were holding your lighter up at a gig or maybe you were dancing to Candy! There's that moment when you're so aligned with someone and it gives us this buzz of energy right? We can do that in our classroom. Remember that class I talked about in Chapter 3? It was like a full-blown riot after lunch. Children would be shouting at each other, shouting at me, trying to tell me what happened. The energy was so heightened I felt like I needed a fire extinguisher. When I started singing with them after lunch I honestly felt pure magic in the air. All singing as one. By the time we had finished, everyone was so connected that the conflicts they had at lunch didn't seem to matter any more. In another class I did this first thing in the morning. I remember singing 'Rise Up' and it was such a powerful way to start the day. Children were all singing to each other and felt such a sense of community. I remember I played it on the last day of school and children started crying because it was so nostalgic of our classroom family. Here is a bank of ideas to activate the energy in your room through collective synchrony:

- singing (obvs)
- dancing (guided dances are great for this like Kidz Bop!)
- clapping
- chanting
- yoga (Cosmic Kids is great for this!)
- movement meditation (Go Noodle 'Flow' is perfect!)

Settlers

As you have probably guessed, settlers are all about bringing the heart rate down through calming practices. This is linked to the parasympathetic response which is part of the nervous system. Its job is to **relax or reduce your body's activities**. These types of activities are perfect if you or your class are feeling overheated. For me, a key variable here is the environment. How can I adapt the environment to bring a collective sense of calm and slow down the pace? One thing I do is turn the lights off or close the blinds. Naturally, lights on are linked to being alert so when we remove this it supports our eyes to have a sensory rest and this signals that feeling across our mind and body too. Another thing I am a little bit obsessed with is music. I use music religiously in my classroom because it is so influential for our mood. I personally like a bit of piano instrumental. The Calm app (www.calm.com) is a great addition for the classroom too! There are lots of ideas in Chapter 5, 'Behaviour and the classroom', when you look at the calm space section. Here is an overview of ideas:

- breathing breaks!
- guided meditation (there are so many kid-friendly ones online)
- colouring, dot to dots or wordsearches

- kinetic sand, play-dough or Lego
- reading café (I like to invite children to take their shoes off and sit or lay however they like)
- go outside!
- sensory bucket fillers like wall pushes or ear lobe rubbing

The key here is these are **FOR YOU** too. At the moment, I am a specialist teacher so I work across different classes. In one day I teach across six classes. This can be quite unsettling for me so I start all of my lessons with the same routine: a story with the lights off, a movement activity or game and a breathing activity. This week a teaching assistant said to me 'I really like that you know. I think it helps me!' And I was like, yeah babe. That is why I do it! It was mainly for me ha! It is all about ensuring I have a super positive start to a session by supporting myself and bringing the class together.

Affirmations

Emily talks about affirmations as a way of 'doubling down' on the experience you have created with your class. Rather than just experiencing it. SAY IT. Say how it feels. Say how you feel about them. Be in that moment and let it take up space.

> ### SCRIPT SNIP
>
> *That was so beautiful to watch my heart is filled with joy!*
> *That was so fun, I feel so happy to be here with you doing this.*
> *That was so special, thank you for all participating in that, my heart is dancing now!*
> *That was so calming, my body feels so relaxed. I love experiencing that with you!*

So what does it all sound like together?

Ok, remember that reflection you jotted down earlier? We are going to revisit that now with everything we have learnt. How could you respond to that particular situation? DON'T WORRY. I will go first. So, if you remember, mine was about feeling anxious for classroom visitors and I started feeling impatient. Now, since I was feeling anxious a settler practice would be great here. So bringing that all together with a script:

How do I feel? What shall we do?

I am not saying you need to tell them your life story about what you are feeling. They don't need to hear about the argument you had with your partner this morning. Just sharing how your body is feeling is perfect! Ok. Ready? Your turn …

In the box below, note down and consider: *How do you feel? What do you think you should do?*

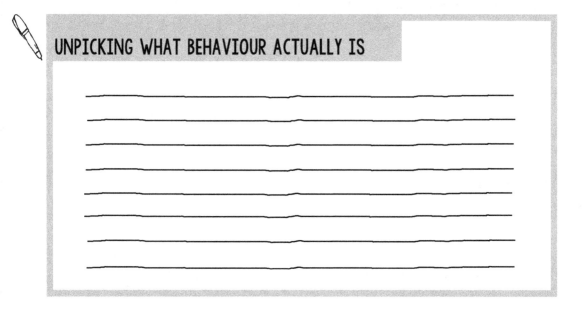

UNPICKING WHAT BEHAVIOUR ACTUALLY IS

Get your sensory on!

Do you know what we need to normalise? Sensory tools for adults. You know, when I led my first staff meeting I was TERRIFIED. Instinctually, I tore some Blu Tack off my wall and rubbed it in my fingers throughout. I needed to divert the energy. I needed something EXTRA to support myself and ground myself in that moment. There will be days when you need something extra. Some days are harder than others. USE it. Use a squeezy ball or a thumb stone. Use a marble mover or a piece of play-dough. Support yourself.

A word of caution

These are everyday strategies to support us for the range of emotions that pop us. Experiencing a range of emotions is normal. However, if you feel that you are feeling overheated or low battery all day every day I would urge you to seek support. If you feel that you are struggling to cope or the feelings are too overwhelming, please don't think you need to *figure it out*. Ask for help.

Practise what you ~~preach~~ teach.

TAKEAWAY BAG

- Our wellbeing impacts our classroom management.
- If we don't respond to our needs we are likely to have a further negative experience with behaviour and possibly lead to burnout.
- Identifying how we feel and our triggers is essential to responding to our needs.
- There is a range of activities we can do to support ourselves in the classroom.
- Bringing children together in synchrony is our super power.
- Normalise talking about how you feel to your children and modelling what you need.
- Ask for help if you need it.

LIGHTS, CAMERA, ACTION REFLECTION

LIGHTS

What stood out to you in this chapter?

CAMERA

What does this look like for you right now? Tomorrow?

ACTION REFLECTION

What do you want to learn more about? What do you want to develop further?

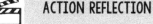

CHAPTER 15

Behaviour: The discovered modules

'I wonder if there is a school of unlearning.'

(Mackesy 2022)

Babe. You made it. The fact that you made it here shows me (and you, more importantly) that you are a committed, passionate and reflective educator. Unlearning and relearning is not a simple process. It's conflicting, confusing and at times even irritating! I hear you. I've been there and continue to keep learning so I know it can be a lot to grapple with. What now?

Let's talk about the 1 per cent rule (Finnis 2021). When making big shifts in culture and mindset, it can seem incredibly overwhelming. The 1 per cent rule puts this into perspective. Rather than trying to change everything all at once, what if we just tweaked our practice by 1 per cent every day? It might be deciding to prioritise your visual timetables. It could be launching a calm space, check-ins or planning for emotional vaccines. Whatever it is. Just pick one thing. And you know what? After 100 days, you will have made 100 per cent progress. 1 per cent every day. So? Make a pledge to yourself now. What is the first thing you are going to do?

'Being kind to yourself is one of the greatest kindnesses' said the mole.

(Mackesy 2022)

I want you to promise yourself something now. Promise you will be kind to yourself. The last thing the education system needs is a dose of shame, guilt or pressure. Don't put it all on your shoulders. We can't change the whole system, but we can change 1 per cent every day. Focus on one step at a time, not the whole staircase.

If you do find yourself overwhelmed with behaviour, seek help. Don't second guess it. This book is to provide you with insight and practical strategies but I am not in the classroom with you. I don't know your context or the specific children in your class. Seek professional help if you feel like you are struggling. Not just for yourself, for your children. There's no pride in buying a ticket to burnout. Let's normalise asking for help.

You are officially a part of the movement. The movement that wants to revolutionise how we view behaviour in schools. The movement that wants every child to thrive. No matter what. And the movement that never stops learning to achieve that. I'm so glad you're here.

To join a community of educators who feel the same way, come and find me @goodmorningmsfosterltd on Instagram and let's connect!

'Sometimes I think you believe in me more than I do,' said the boy.

'You'll catch up,' said the horse.

(Mackesy 2022)

One more for the road …

LIGHTS, CAMERA, ACTION REFLECTION

LIGHT

What stood out to you in this book?

CAMERA

What does this look like for you right now? Tomorrow?

ACTION REFLECTION

What do you want to learn more about? What do you want to develop further?

Thank you for being here and thank you for being you.
Lots of love,
Jen

References

Adams, M. (2012) *What are the Essential Components of an I-Message?* Gordon Training International. Available here: www.gordontraining.com/leadership/what-are-the-essential-components-of-an-i-message/

Ageing Better (2019) *The Role of Food in Building Connections and Relationships*. London: National Lottery Community Fund. Available here: www.tnlcommunityfund.org.uk/media/documents/ageing-better/Ageing-Better-Role-of-Food-in-Building-Connections-and-Relationships.pdf?mtime=20190514094521

Badu, O. (2023) *How to Build Your Antiracist Classroom*. London: Sage.

Baldwin, J. (1961) *Nobody Knows My Name: Fifth Avenue, Uptown: A Letter from Harlem*. New York: Dial Press.

Bateman, C. (2022) Nearly half of teachers plan to quit by 2027 due to workload, survey finds. *Sky News*. Available here: news.sky.com/story/nearly-half-of-teachers-plan-to-quit-by-2027-due-to-workload-survey-finds-12587989

Bomber, L.M. (2020) *Know Me to Teach Me: Differentiated Discipline for Those Recovering from Adverse Childhood Experience*. Broadway: Worth.

Bowyer-Crane, C., Bonetti, S., Tracey, L. and Nielson, D. (2022) The truth about how Covid has impacted on school staff. *TES*. Available here: www.tes.com/magazine/analysis/early-years/covid-school-staff-teachers-wellbeing-mental-health

Brown, E. (2016) Yale study suggests racial bias among preschool teachers. *Washington Post*. Available here: www.washingtonpost.com/news/education/wp/2016/09/27/yale-study-suggests-racial-bias-among-preschool-teachers/

Brunzell, T. and Norrish, J. (2021) *Creating Trauma-Informed, Strengths-Based Classrooms: Teacher Strategies for Nurturing Students' Healing, Growth, and Learning*. London: Jessica Kingsley.

Cell Press (2021) People synchronize heart rates while listening attentively to stories. *ScienceDaily*. Available here: www.sciencedaily.com/releases/2021/09/210914111238.htm#:~:text=a%20personal%20conversation.-,According%20to%20a%20new%20study%2C%20subjects'%20heart%20rates%20synchronize%20even,in%20the%20journal%20Cell%20Reports

Commission on Young Lives (2022) *All Together Now. Inclusion Not Exclusion: Supporting All Young People to Succeed in School*. Available here: thecommissiononyounglives.co.uk/wp-content/uploads/2022/04/COYL-Education-report-FINAL-APR-29-2022.pdf

Conkbayir, M. (2021) *Early Childhood and Neuroscience: Theory, Research and Implications for Practice*. London: Bloomsbury.

Delahooke, M. (2020) *Beyond Behaviours: Using Brain Science and Compassion to Understand and Solve Children's Behavioural Challenges*. London: John Murray Learning.

Dweck, C. (2017) *Mindset – Updated Edition: Changing The Way You think To Fulfil Your Potential*. London: Robinson.

Finnis, M. (2021) *Independent Thinking on Restorative Practice: Building Relationships, Improving Behaviour and Creating Stronger Communities*. Carnarvon: Independent Thinking Press.

Gilbert, L., Gus, L. and Rose, J. (2021) *Emotion Coaching with Children and Young People in Schools: Promoting Positive Behaviour, Wellbeing and Resilience*. London: Jessica Kingsley.

Gillborn, D. and Demack, S. (2018) *Exclusions Review 2018 Evidence on the Exclusion of Black Caribbean and Mixed: White/Black Caribbean Students*. University of Birmingham Centre for Research in Race and Education. Available here: councilmeetings.lewisham.gov.uk/documents/s61052/Exclusions%20Appendix%20B%20CRRE%20Uni%20of%20Birmingham%20Exclusions%20Review%20Race.pdf

Goleman, D. (2020) *Emotional Intelligence: 25th Anniversary Edition*. London: Bloomsbury.

gov.UK (2020) School teacher workforce. *Ethnicity Facts and Figures Service Report*. Available here: www.ethnicity-facts-figures.service.gov.uk/workforce-and-business/workforce-diversity/school-teacher-workforce/latest

Grierson, J. (2020) Nine out of 10 children on remand in London come from BAME background. *Guardian*. Available here: www.theguardian.com/society/2020/dec/21/nine-out-of-10-children-on-remand-in-london-come-from-bame-background

Guest, K. (2017) Interview: Matt Haig: 'I think books can save us. They sort of saved me.' *Guardian*. Available here: www.theguardian.com/books/2017/jun/30/matt-haig-interview-books-saved-me

Hepburn, E. (2023) *A Toolkit for Your Emotions: 45 Ways to Feel Better*. London: Greenfinch.

Hickey, G. (Kinesophy) (2022) *Myokines: Connecting Movement, Muscles and Well-Being*. Available here: kinesophy.com/myokines-connecting-movement-muscles-and-well-being/

Jennings, P. and Siegal, D. (2015) *Mindfulness for Teachers: Simple Skills for Peace and Productivity in the Classroom*. New York: W.W. Norton.

Keeler, J., Roth, E., Nauser, B., Spitsbergen, J., Waters, D. and Vianney J. (2015) The neurochemistry and the social flow of singing: bonding and oxytocin. *Frontiers in Human Neuroscience*, 9(518). Available here: www.frontiersin.org/articles/10.3389/fnhum.2015.00518/full

Kennedy, B. (2022) *Good Inside: A Practical Guide to Becoming the Parent You Want to Be*. London: Thorsons.

Klein, A. (2021) 1,500 decisions a day (at least!): how teachers cope with a dizzying array of questions. *Education Week*. Available here: www.edweek.org/teaching-learning/

1-500-decisions-a-day-at-least-how-teachers-cope-with-a-dizzying-array-of-questions/2021/12#:~:text=How%20many%20decisions%20do%20teachers,cited%20in%20education%20circles%20today

Kohn, A. (2015) *Punished by Rewards: Twenty-Fifth Anniversary Edition: The Trouble with Gold Stars, Incentive Plans, A's, Praise, and Other Bribes*. New York: HarperOne.

Lastiri, L. (2021) *What Happens in the Brain While Reading?* Available here: irisreading.com/what-happens-in-the-brain-while-reading/#:~:text=As%20you%20read%2C%20your%20brain's,and%20use%20and%20comprehend%20grammar

Lloyd, T. (2021) *'Slant' Won't Work for SEND Students, So What Does?* ADHD Foundation. Available here: www.adhdfoundation.org.uk/2021/09/13/slant-wont-work-for-send-students-so-what-does/

Mackesy, C. (2022) *The Boy, the Mole, the Fox and the Horse: The Animated Story*. London: Ebury Press.

Mahon, L. (2022) Mixed race Caribbean girls three times more likely to be excluded. *Voice Online*. Available here: www.voice-online.co.uk/news/uk-news/2022/09/23/mixed-race-caribbean-girls-three-times-more-likely-to-be-excluded/

Maslow, A.H. (1943) A theory of human motivation. *Psychological Review*, *50*(4), 430–437.

Moore, C. (2019) *What is Negativity Bias and how can it be Overcome?* Positive Psychology.com. Available here: positivepsychology.com/3-steps-negativity-bias/#:~:text=References-,What%20Is%20Negativity%20Bias%3F,383)

Mayo Clinic (2022) Exercise and stress: Get moving to manage stress. *Worldwide: Mayo Clinic*. Available here: www.mayoclinic.org/healthy-lifestyle/stress-management/in-depth/exercise-and-stress/art-20044469#:~:text=Physical%20activity%20may%20help%20bump,contribute%20to%20this%20same%20feeling

McIntyre, N., Parveen, N. and Thomas, T. (2021) Exclusion rates five times higher for Black Caribbean pupils in part of England. *Guardian*. Available here: www.theguardian.com/education/2021/mar/24/exclusion-rates-black-caribbean-pupils-england

Miller, C. (2022) *How Trauma Affects Kids in School*. Child Mind Institute. Available here: childmind.org/article/how-trauma-affects-kids-school/

Murphy, K. (2022) *A Guide to SEND in the Early Years: Supporting Children with Special Educational Needs and Disabilities*. London: Featherstone.

NASEN (2021) *Exclusion Data Released*. Available here: nasen.org.uk/news/exclusion-data-released

NEU (2020) *NEU Comment on Exclusions*. Available here: policymogul.com/key-updates/10360/neu-comment-on-exclusions

Nickerson, C. (2021) Emotional contagion. *Simply Psychology*. Available here: www.simplypsychology.org/what-is-emotional-contagion.html

Ostrowski, R. and Palladino, C. (2021) *Addie's Me Cave*. Published by Cheryl Palladino, Rachael Ostrowski.

Payne Bryson, T. and Siegal, D. (2012) *The Whole-Brain Child: 12 Proven Strategies to Nurture Your Child's Developing Mind*. London: Robinson.

Pearce, K. (2019) *Mirror Neurons: Why Good Stories Provoke Empathy and Connection*. Available here: www.diygenius.com/mirror-neurons/#:~:text=The%20proponents%20 of%20the%20mirror,are%20happy%2C%20we%20feel%20happy

Pillay, S. (2016) *How Simply Moving Benefits your Mental Health*. Massachusetts: Harvard Health. Available here: www.health.harvard.edu/blog/how-simply-moving-benefits-your-mental-health-201603289350

Pink, H. (2018) *Drive: The Surprising Truth About What Motivates Us*. Edinburgh: Cannongate.

Plevin, R. (2017) *Attention-Grabbing Starters and Plenaries for Teachers: 99 Outrageously Engaging Activities to Increase Student Participation and Make Learning Fun* (Needs-Focused Teaching Resource). Penrith: Life Raft Media.

Plevin, R. (2019) *Take Control of the Noisy Class: Chaos to Calm in 15 Second*. Cumbria: Life Raft Media.

Powell, A. (2018) When science meets mindfulness: Researchers study how it seems to change the brain in depressed patients. *Harvard Gazette*. Available here: news.harvard. edu/gazette/story/2018/04/harvard-researchers-study-how-mindfulness-may-change-the-brain-in-depressed-patients/

Radford, L., Corral, S., Bradley, C., Fisher, H., Bassett, C., Howat, N. and Collishaw, S. (2011) *Child Abuse and Neglect in the UK Today: Research into the Prevalence of Child Maltreatment in the United Kingdom*. London: NSPCC. Available here: learning.nspcc. org.uk/research-resources/pre-2013/child-abuse-neglect-uk-today

raisingchildren.net.au (2022) *Neurodiversity and Neurodivergence: A Guide for Families*. Available here: raisingchildren.net.au/guides/a-z-health-reference/neurodiversity-neu-rodivergence-guide-for-families#:~:text=About%201%20in%205%2D6,can%20be%20 described%20as%20neurodivergent

Reid, N. (2020) Not all superheroes wear capes: how you have the power to change the world. TEDxFrankfurt. *Available here:* www.ted.com/talks/nova_reid_not_all_superhe-roes_wear_capes_you_have_the_power_to_change_the_world?language=en

Robinson, L., Smith, M. and Segal, J. (2022) *Laughter is the Best Medicine*. Available here: www.helpguide.org/articles/mental-health/laughter-is-the-best-medicine. htm#:~:text=Laughter%20triggers%20the%20release%20of,can%20even%20temporar-ily%20relieve%20pain

Seligman, M. (2011) *Flourish: A New Understanding of Happiness and Well-Being - and How To Achieve Them*. Massachusetts: Nicholas Brealey.

Shashkevich, A. (2019) The power of language: How words shape people, culture. *Stanford News*. Available here: news.stanford.edu/2019/08/22/the-power-of-language-how-words-shape-people-culture/

Silverton, K. (2021) *There's No Such Thing As 'Naughty': The Groundbreaking Guide for Parents with Children aged 0–5*. London: Piatkus.

Smith, D. (2015) *Better Than Carrots or Sticks: Restorative Practices for Positive Classroom Management*. Virginia: ASCD.

Sobel, D. and Alston, S. (2021) *The Inclusive Classroom: A New Approach to Differentiation*. London: Bloomsbury.

The Stable Company (2020) *SEND Children 'five times more likely to be excluded'.* Available here: www.thestablecompany.com/blog/sen-children-five-times-more-likely-to-be-excluded

Steiner, C. (2003) *Emotional Literacy: Intelligence with a Heart.* California: Personhood Press.

StudyMoose (2016) *Jacob Kounin on Behavior in the Classroom.* Available at: studymoose.com/jacob-kounin-on-behavior-in-the-classroom-essay

Waldinger, R. (2015) What makes a good life? Lessons from the longest study on happiness. Brookline Massachusetts: TED Conference. *Available here:* www.ted.com/talks/robert_waldinger_what_makes_a_good_life_lessons_from_the_longest_study_on_happiness/transcript?language=en

Wallace, I. (2014) *Talk-Less Teaching: Practice, Participation and Progress.* Carmarthen: Crown House.

Weimer, M. (2015) The power of language to influence thought and action. *Faculty Focus.* Available here: www.facultyfocus.com/articles/effective-teaching-strategies/the-power-of-language-to-influence-thought-and-action/#:~:text=Language%20influences%20thought%20and,related%20to%20teaching%20and%20learning

Wittgenstein, L. (1889–1951) *Tractatus Logico-Philosophicus* [reprinted, with a few corrections]. New York: Harcourt, Brace, 1933.

World Economic Forum (2020) Study: Almost All Black British Children Have Experienced Racism at School. *Available here:* www.weforum.org/agenda/2020/11/racism-united-kingdom-schools-black-children-inequality/

Young, Y. (2016) Teachers' implicit bias against Black students starts in preschool, study finds. *Guardian.* Available here: www.theguardian.com/world/2016/oct/04/black-students-teachers-implicit-racial-bias-preschool-study

Index

1 per cent rule, 186
4 Ps, of successful routines, 101–102
4 Rs, 115–116
5 Ls of learning, 162

ableism, 161
academic needs, 58–60
acknowledgement, 28
activators, 180, 181–182
Addie's Me Cave (2021), 64
adultification, 142
adverse childhood experience (ACE), 124, 125, 127
affirmations, 181, 183
amygdala, 2–3
    alarm, 3–5
    hijack, 3
    informant, 3
anti-racism, 143
attendance, 76
attention
    getters, 102
    seeking, 18
Autism Level Up, 65
autonomy, 92–93

Badu, Orlene, 138, 143, 146
BAE (basic needs, academic needs, emotional needs)
    classrooms, 55–63
basic needs, in the classroom, 55–58
'Becoming an Anti-Racist Educator' podcast, 142
behaviour
    and bias, 138–147
    boiling pot, 36–37
    challenging, 19
    charts, 165–166
    and classroom, 53–68
    and classroom management, 95–106
    and connection, 22–34
    and consequences, 107–122
    discovered modules, 186–187
    and emotions, 7, 36–52
    goldilocks, 90–92

'hunger games', 92–93
and language, 15–21
and learning, 84–94
low-level, 18–19
myths about, 1–2
and neurodiversity, 159–172
as neurological response, 2–3
'no' behaviour, 85–86
'offline' behaviour, 88–89
and restorative practice, 148–158
and rewards, 69–83
stems from feelings and needs, 7–8
tracing, 85
and trauma, 123–137
volcano, 37–38
'wiggle wiggle' behaviour, 89–90
and you, 173–185
behaviour management
    and behaviour support, 80, 81
    and classroom management, 79
behaviourism, 73
bias, and behaviour, 138–147
body, 38–39
    check chart, 169–170
    language, 103–104
    scans, 146
Bomber, Louise Michelle, 110–111
brain, handy model of, 6–7
breathing
    boards, 62
    technique, 50, 131
Brown, Allison R., 140

Calm app, 182
calm pass, 64–65
CALM scripts, 119
calm spaces, in classroom, 61–62, 64, 168–169
'the carrot and the stick' concept, 69
certificates and points, 72
chair-based learning, 164
challenging behaviour, 19
check-ins, 47–48, 63, 65

child-centred planning and ideas, 33
child-centred routines, 34
Child Mind Institute, 127
choice board, 63
classroom
  academic needs, 58–60
  BAE, 55–63
  basic needs, 55–58
  and behaviour, 53–68
  emotional needs, 61–63
classroom management
  attention getters, 102
  and behaviour, 95–106
  and behaviour management, 79
  body language, 103–104
  classroom jobs, 101
  classroom set-up, 99
  reading the needs, 103
  routines, 100
  timers, 105
  visual timetables, 105
  visuals, 104–105
co-regulation, 44, 129, 136, 169
cognitively demanding, 37
communicative tools, 134–135
competition, 75, 92
connection
  control vs, 75
  cultivating, 181
  seeking, 18
  social, 25
connection, building, 22–34
  with acknowledgement, 28
  with empathy, 28–29
  with endorphins, 27
  with food, eating together, 25–26
  with fun and imagination, 29–30
  with meaningful questions, 31–32
  with oxytocin, 26–27
  with positive affirmations, 32
  with positive feedback, 30–31
  on their turf, 26
connectors, 180
consequences
  behaviour and, 107–122
  CALM scripts, 119
  emotional support, 117
  exception files, 112
  FAQs, 121–122
  guard dog and, 111
  ladders, 117–118
  positive response, 115–116
  removing play, 112
  in schools, 108–111
  skills teaching, 114–115

time out, 111
  trauma and, 130–131
  why question, 113–114
consistency, 76
  vs let it go, 105–106
  vs predictability, 132–133
control
  vs connection, 75
  vs motivation, 74
Creating Trauma-Informed, Strengths-Based
    Classrooms (2021), 124, 127
curiosity, 146, 169
curriculum, 144

Daniels, Emily, 173, 176, 180, 183
Delahooke, Mona, 126, 127
distressed behaviour, 19
doodling, 63
dynamic seating, 167
dysregulation, 44

ear defenders and eye masks, 63
emotional awareness scale, 45
emotional contagion, 85
emotional intelligence, 41–42
emotional literacy, 42
emotional literacy books, 48–49
emotional needs, in the classroom, 61–63
emotional regulation, 129
emotional support, 117
emotional tool
  breathing, 50
  check-ins, 47–48
  emotional literacy books, 48–49
  emotional vaccines, 50
  modelling, 49
emotional vaccines, 50, 114–115
emotions
  and behaviour, 7, 36–52
  myths, 51
  negative and positive, 51
  and time out, 50–51
Emotions Shelf, 49
empathy, 28–29
endorphins, 27
engagement-driven strategies, 89
equity and assumptions, 145
esteem, 7
exception files, 112
extrinsic motivation, 92

feedback, 171
feel better effect, 27
feelings boards, 63
fight/flight responses, 3, 129

Finnis, Mark, 154
Flood, David, 171
Flood, Justin P., 171
Foster Formulas, 9, 34, 109, 113, 177

generational trauma, 143
The Girl Who Thought in Pictures (Grandin), 171
goldilocks behaviour, 90–92
Goleman, Daniel, 3
Gordon, Thomas, 179
Grandin, Temple, 171
greetings, 28
growth mindset, 86
guard dog and consequences, 111

Haig, Matt, 49
handy model of the brain, 6–7
Hepburn, Emma, 1, 3, 6, 7, 36–38, 52
hippocampus, 2–3
homework, 77
'hunger games' behaviour, 92–93

I-messaging and modelling, 179–180
iceberg model, 7–13
identity, 139
    and role models, 144
If–Then rewards, 77
intrinsic motivation, 92
'is' to 'is presenting', 19

Jennings, Patricia, 176

Kennedy, Becky, 50, 113, 115
A Kid's Book About Autism (Flood), 171
Kohn, Alfie, 73–74
Kounin, Jacob, 177

Laleiu, Ginny, 119
language
    and behaviour, 15–21
    in schools, 17
language-centred teaching, 166
laziness, 18
learning, 166
    5 Ls of, 162
    and behaviour, 84–94
    chair-based, 164
    and rewards, 76
listening, 29, 77, 162–164
logical and natural consequences, 122
love and belonging, 7
low-level behaviour, 18–19

Makaton signing, 134
manipulation, 18

Maslow, A.H., 7
mastery, 92–93
McNeil, Rosamund, 144
microaggressions, 142
mindfulness, 44
mirroring, 150
modelling, 49, 64
mood zones, 168
motivation, control vs, 74
movement, 167–168, 187
Murphy, Kerry, 159, 162, 164, 168, 169, 171
My Mind is Full, 64
myokines, 27
myths
    about children's behaviour, 1–2
    emotion and, 51

needs
    physiological/safety, 7
    reading the, 103
    See also classroom
neuro-affirming approaches, 161, 162, 165, 166, 169
neuroception, 125
neurodivergence, 58, 126, 161, 162, 169
neurodiversity, 159–172
neuroscience, 1, 29
neurotypical behaviours, 161, 165, 171
'no thinking' task, 74
non-verbal signals, 134
Norrish, Jacolyn, 124
Now–That rewards, 77–78

observational awareness, 135
'offline' behaviour, 88–89
Ostrowski, Rachael, 64
oxytocin, 26–27

Palladino, Cheryl, 64
physiological needs, 7
piggy bank analogy, 25–34
Pink, Daniel H., 74, 92
play, 29–30
play-dough, 62
play time, 112
Plevin, Rob, 90
point system, 72
positive affirmations, 32
positive feedback, 30–31
practices, defined, 180–181
pre-frontal cortex, 2–3, 5, 6, 174
predictability and consistency, 132–133
proactivity, 146
Punished by Rewards (2015), 73
pupil shout-outs, 34
purpose, 92–93

racial bias, 141
raffles, 72
reading, 28–29, 63, 76
Regulated Classroom©, 173, 180, 181
regulation, 43
Reid, Nova, 142
relationships, building, 23, 27–28, 29
restorative conversation, 63, 153–158
    impact of, 156–157
    structure of, 154
    tips for, 157–158
restorative practice
    and behaviour, 148–158
    ideas to understanding, 150–153
    to real life, 149
    reasons for, 149
rewards
    and behaviour, 69–83
    competition, 75
    consistency, 76
    control vs connection, 75
    control vs motivation, 74
    expecting every time, 75
    going the distance, 74–75
    If–Then rewards, 77
    and learning, 76
    life without, 78
    Now–That rewards, 77–78
    supporting outcomes, 74
    at their worst/best, 76–78
role models, identity and, 144
routines, 100

safety needs, 7
school-to-prison-pipeline, 110–111
Seigel, Daniel, 43
self-actualization, 7
self-regulation, 5, 44
sensory timer, 63
settlers, 181, 182–183
Siegel, Daniel, 6, 111, 129, 130, 177–179
singing, 26–27

skills teaching, 114–115
SLANT, 162–163
social connections, 25
spelling test, 76–77
Steiner, Claude, 45
storytelling, 29
stress response, 3, 124
structured choices, 133

tactile body language, 164–165
time out, 50–51, 111
timers, 105
toxic stress, 125
trauma
    and behaviour, 123–137
    co-regulation, 136
    and consequences, 130–131
    description, 124
    focus on predictability and consistency, 132–133
    generational, 143
    impact on brain, 126
    observational awareness, 135
    providing communicative tools, 134–135
    providing structured choices, 133
    rebuilding sense of safety in relationships, 132
    supporting yourself, 131–132
Truman Show, 162

unsettled behaviour, 18–19

visual timetables, 66, 105, 167
visuals, 104–105
volcano model, 37–38

Waldinger, Robert, 24
Wallace, Isabella, 89
weather charts, 71
whole-body listening, 162–164
'wiggle wiggle' behaviour, 89–90
window of tolerance, 43, 125, 129
withitness and tracking, 177
Wittgenstein, L., 17